SRI CHAKRA YANTRA

Manifest anything with the symbol of everything

VINITA RASHINKAR

INDIA • SINGAPORE • MALAYSIA

Notion Press

Old No. 38, New No. 6
McNichols Road, Chetpet
Chennai - 600 031

First Published by Notion Press 2019
Copyright © Vinita Rashinkar 2019
All Rights Reserved.

ISBN 978-1-64587-640-3

This book has been published with all efforts taken to make the material error-free after the consent of the author. However, the author and the publisher do not assume and hereby disclaim any liability to any party for any loss, damage, or disruption caused by errors or omissions, whether such errors or omissions result from negligence, accident, or any other cause.

While every effort has been made to avoid any mistake or omission, this publication is being sold on the condition and understanding that neither the author nor the publishers or printers would be liable in any manner to any person by reason of any mistake or omission in this publication or for any action taken or omitted to be taken or advice rendered or accepted on the basis of this work. For any defect in printing or binding the publishers will be liable only to replace the defective copy by another copy of this work then available.

For Puja and Amit

CONTENTS

1.	Introduction	7
2.	The Sri Chakra Yantra – King of all Yantras	13
3.	Shaktism, Tantra and Sri Vidya	31
4.	Sri Chakra and the Human Body	71
	a. Sri Chakra and Healing	80
	b. Sri Chakra and the Pineal Gland	82
5.	Sounds of the Sri Chakra	87
6.	Mudras for relaxation	193
7.	Sattvic Lifestyle for the Sri Chakra Yantra practitioner	203
8.	Simple ritual worship of the Sri Chakra Yantra	217
References		*229*
Acknowledgements		*231*

1
INTRODUCTION

Manifest anything using the symbol of everything

"Everything is energy and that's all there is to it. Match the frequency of the reality you want and you cannot help but get that reality. It can be no other way. This is not philosophy. This is physics."

– Albert Einstein

We are all constantly manifesting; we are just not aware of it. Our current situation in life can be traced directly back to our thoughts and feelings that we have experienced at some point in time in the past. We are shaping our own reality, unconsciously or consciously, all the time. Remember how as children we would say "I want to be a scientist" or "I want to be an author"; today we may be a scientist or an author or whoever we wanted to be when we were little. This is an example of unconsciously manifesting based on our upbringing, belief systems and outcome of our conditioned mind.

We can also manifest with determination and by working towards a goal when we set our minds to something (studying for a degree, saving to build up a house) or we can consciously manifest when we come to a realization that it is possible to connect with and tap directly into a higher energy, which then empowers us by turning on our deepest inner potential. Conscious manifestation is about creating what we desire with a clear vision, deep belief and absolute awareness and appreciation of the fact that there is an unseen force that will guide us to our goal(s).

All spiritual traditions have upheld the belief that everything in the cosmos is energy (it is called chi, qi, prana, etc., in different cultures) and that every aspect of existence is deeply interwoven in this giant web of energy.

Modern advances in science, especially studies in Quantum Mechanics, have led to a vindication of this long-held belief that "everything is energy" as scientists realized that all particles are merely vibrations of energy. If the universe is pure energy and we are but a small part of this same energy, it then stands to reason that there exists a possibility for us, as individuals, to tune into the frequency of the universe's energy.

There are several methods of tuning in (such as through the power of sound, crystals, meditation, prayer). One such powerful method is by using symbols (such as the Sri Chakra Yantra) as a tuning fork. Just as we are able to tune into a specific channel on television, on the radio, by selecting a particular frequency, these symbols allow us the ability to tune in and engage with the powers of creation in the universe.

So, what exactly is a yantra?

A yantra is a graphic and geometric representation of the Universal energy.

Thoughts and words cannot exist in the spiritual dimension since they are a construct of the intellect and mind. Sacred geometry arises from this fact that many philosophical truths cannot be expressed with words. The world around us is filled with geometrical designs and shapes. Ancient cultures, including those of Greeks, Egyptians, Chinese, Mayans and Hindus, observed that certain geometric patterns are found recurring throughout nature - spirals, hexagons and concentric circles to name a few) - and believed them to be the building blocks of all creation in the universe.

In Hindu Tantra, three kinds of external symbols are used to relate to and connect with the Universal energy.

* An image showing the energy in a human or animal form (such as Krishna, Hanuman or Ganesha)
* A yantra depicting the energy in the form of geometric shapes
* A mantra which is energy in the form of a sound

The word yantra is derived from the root verb "yantr" meaning "to restrain or control." It can be understood as a machine or a device that controls human effort in performing a task by providing assistance. A mantra uses sound energy to bring about a balance between the mind and the body, while a yantra uses the visual medium to bring about a state of equilibrium.

A yantra can work as a transformer of our psychic energies, allowing us a glimpse into the beauty and power of the universe. There are hundreds of yantra designs which are specific to planets, gods and principles. These geometric patterns can be drawn out on the floor in the form of rangoli (kollam), painted on a paper or tree bark, or etched on metal sheets such as copper, silver or gold.

One of the most powerful, auspicious and important yantras in the Tantra tradition is the Sri Chakra Yantra. Known as a "Rajayantra" (or king of yantras), it is a symbol of all energy, power and creativity - hence a symbol of everything. Advaita Vedanta sages have said that this yantra holds the key to mastering the science of Creation (acquiring all that we desire) and Destruction (getting rid of all that we no longer desire).

The Sri Chakra Yantra is believed to have been divinely revealed rather than invented. It is not a creation of human intellect, and the geometry is said to have appeared to "self-realized" yogis in their peak meditative state (samadhi). This supremely powerful symbol is a representation of the infinite power of the Universal energy and is a geometric form of the process of creation itself.

The physical yantra can be used as a tool to turn our every thought into a directive to the universe.

As you channelize your energy to be in synchrony with that of the universe, you will notice that:

* all internal and external roadblocks that have sabotaged your ability to forge ahead will be removed, one by one
* enriching circumstances and opportunities will come your way, helping you move forward on your path(s)

Manifestation is not accomplished by spending hours in the meditation of the yantra but as a result of retraining your everyday thought processes and by merely using the Sri Chakra Yantra as a device to optimally amplify your connection with the universe.

This book is an endeavour to introduce an element of change in your personal thought processes, to help connect with the Universal energy and to manifest your deepest desires.

Any alterations in the personal thought processes can only be embarked upon after gaining a better understanding of two things:

* A better understanding of your body, mind, spirit and your personal routines and ways to improve your quality of life which is covered in the chapters that focus upon the relationship of the human body to the Sri Chakra Yantra and the connection between the Sri Chakra Yantra and the Pineal Gland. There is also a brief note on healing and the Sri Chakra. There is one chapter that deals with mudras and contains details about specific mudras that are commonly used for relaxation and stress management. The book then lays out some pointers to leading a sattvic life. Eventually, we arrive at how to meditate on the Sri Chakra Yantra and use it as a tool for manifestation in the final chapter of the book.
* The metaphysical aspects of life which are reflected in the philosophies underlying Shaktism, Tantra, Dasa Mahavidya and Sri Vidya. Once these concepts throw some light on the basics of the Sri Chakra worship, we then study the nature of sacred geometry and significance, structure and meaning of the Sri Chakra Yantra. This will be followed by an analysis of the use of sounds in the path to spiritual growth. Special attention is given to the sounds (mantras and stotras) associated with the Sri Chakra Yantra.

A fairly large section of this book is dedicated to a detailed explanation and translation of the three most important stotras connected with the Sri Chakra Yantra.

- ✹ Khadgamala
- ✹ Lalita Sahasranama
- ✹ Lalita Trishati

These three stotras play a supremely important role in meditating upon the Sri Chakra Yantra; therefore, you will have to spend some time becoming familiar with them and understanding their meaning and significance.

There has been a huge surge in the popularity of Sri Vidya in recent times and it is a strongly held belief that all the learning pertaining to the Sri Chakra Yantra has to be done under the tutelage of a well-versed guru in the subject. Unfortunately, most of us do not have access to such gurus, who are willing to share their knowledge of this esoteric and mysterious subject to eager learners. All of my learnings about the Sri Chakra Yantra came from self-study and I am more than happy to share it with those with a keen interest in the subject.

My main aim of writing this book is to offer all the information that a novice is seeking to get him/her into the practice of Sri Vidya Sadhana and involve in self-learning rather than seeking it from external sources. The information is laid out in a non-dogmatic manner keeping in mind the practical aspects of modern day living, thereby allowing everyone an opportunity to learn and experience the benefits of the precious Sri Yantra. The process outlined in the book equips you with the skills necessary to harness the tremendous cosmic energies available in the universe and channelize it to make your dreams come true.

This book is not meant to be a comprehensive study of the Sri Chakra. In presenting the Sri Chakra Yantra as a tool for self-development, I have kept in mind the sensibilities of the modern spiritual seeker, your needs and interests, and have desisted from venturing into the realm of mythological references, the inclusion of which would obfuscate and distract the reader from the subject of study. The focus has been to retain only the relevant philosophical allusions that further the understanding of the subject at hand.

All you will need is a 12 x 12 inch print out of the Sri Chakra Yantra (preferably in black and white) and a deep desire to use the powers of this ancient and sacred symbol to lead a more satisfying, wholesome and blissful life.

The Sri Chakra Yantra will have a profound influence on the way you see life and will help you get ahead in both material and spiritual realms. It will help you find clarity of thought, calmness, stability and the ability to manifest all of your desires.

2

THE SRI CHAKRA YANTRA – KING OF ALL YANTRAS

Carl Jung wrote that a man's most vital need is to discover his own reality through the cultivation of a symbolic life: *"Man is in need of a symbolic life. Have you got a corner somewhere in your houses where you perform the rites as you see in India?"*

Archetypes are universal thought forms that are derived from the Collective Unconscious. They can best be described as blueprints of our soul – primordial imprints of consciousness that we are all born with, hardwired in our genes. The Sri Chakra Yantra contains not one but two archetypes – one of symbols or sacred geometry and the other of the universal quest for the quintessential Mother Goddess.

Hinduism is full of ancient and sacred geometric symbols – Om, swastika, linga and vaastu purusha to name a few. They all hold the key(s) to unravelling the secrets of the cosmos. We come across three terms which are commonly used in Hindu symbolism: Mandala, Chakra and Yantra.

The term mandala appears in the Rig Veda and is used generically to stand for any drawing, diagram or geometric pattern that represents the cosmos symbolically or metaphysically.

Example of a Mandala

One of the chief purposes of the mandala is to represent the different layers of the universe – the spiritual realm, the environment we live in and the inner experience of man – and how each of these layers can flow into and out of the next. Therefore, the mandala is perhaps the most essential tool for practitioners seeking to make a spiritual connection.

The Sanskrit word "chakra" essentially denotes a spinning vortex or wheel. In *The Tantra of Sri Chakra Bhavanopanishat* by Prof. S.K. Ramachandra Rao, he writes:

The etymology of the word would suggest that by which anything is done (*kriyate aneana*). The wheel of the cart, the wheel of the potter and the wheel-like weapon that is flung against the enemy are all called 'chakras.' In its extended meaning, chakra also signifies a kingdom because the wheels of the king's chariot can roll in there without hindrance. The king of the land is thus described as 'chakra-vartin.'

The word also signifies arrangement of the army in specific order (*chakravyuha*) to fortify its position and secure victory. Sanskrit poets are found to employ characteristically circular patterns of letters of words (*chakrabandha*) to convey the meaning more forcefully (also more tortuously) than usual.

Whatever the sense in which the word is employed, it invariably means a 'power field,' an arrangement of parts so as to accomplish the desired end. The circular form which the chakra usually brings to mind denotes both comprehension and facility. It comprehends all the parts, units and details in a compact and effective manner so that the whole form is unitary and functional. But the form need not necessarily be circular. The idea of comprehension may be metaphorical, as in expressions like '*ritu-chakra*' (the round of the seasons), '*nakshatra chakra*' (the collection of stars) and '*nadi chakra*' (the arrangement of the arteries).

The most common form of mandala is the powerful, mystical, esoteric and compelling 'yantra.' It is said that Lord Shiva created 64 yantras and gave them to mankind to help them progress materially and spiritually. A yantra is considered to be the residence of its personal deity (*ishta-devata*); therefore, there are yantras named after specific desires and specific gods and goddesses and are a representation of the energies they signify and embody. For example:

Ganesha Yantra – to clear obstacles and succeed in fresh ventures

Kali Yantra – to strengthen the feminine energy and become fearless

Lakshmi Yantra – to acquire material wealth

Dhanvantari Yantra – for healing diseases and good health

Navagraha Yantra – for general prosperity and to balance the chakras

Ganesha Yantra

Kali Yantra

Lakshmi Yantra

Juan Carlos Ramchandani explains "Each yantra is a mantra (sacred phoneme) by means of which the individual mind calls upon the cosmic energy through the three bodies: causal, subtle and material. In addition, the yantras are complemented with mantras, since they combine the power of the practitioner with that of the yantra, which, in turn, vibrates with the infinite power of the universe. In meditation, both instruments are used simultaneously. A properly energized yantra contains the same energy of divinity and is the essence of the divinity."

Every yantra has to conform to three basic principles:

Akriti-rupa or Form

Kriya-rupa or Function

Shakti-rupa or Power

Through constant ritualistic worship, a yantra sheds its dormancy and becomes emblematic of spiritual power. The yantra, therefore, moves from a mere form and function to become a power-diagram.

Yantras are classified according to their uses as below:

Type of Yantra	Its uses
Sharira Yantra	Yantras for the body such as the chakras
Dharana Yantra	Those which are worn on the body to offer protection, ward off disease, etc., such as medallions and talismans
Asan Yantra	Those placed under the seat of a deity or meditation mat, or under the ground before the construction of a building, temple, etc.
Mandala Yantra	A live yantra formed by 9 persons with 8 sitting in 8 cardinal directions and one in the centre to perform the puja or worship
Puja Yantra	Yantras, installed in temples, homes or offices, to which regular worship is offered
Chattar Yantra	Those that are kept under a turban, hat, cap or in the pocket
Darshan Yantra	Yantra, believed to bring good fortune upon its viewer, are placed in temple, home or office

The geometric symmetry that lies within a yantra is a reflection of the unity of the individual with the universe, and the pattern of repetition of seeing the microcosm in the macrocosm and vice versa is said to bring about a balance in the two hemispheres of the brain.

Recent studies have shown that merely looking at certain geometric patterns can alter brain waves and open gateways to higher states of consciousness. The reason why this can happen is that the geometric patterns bring about an alignment of the left and right aspects of the brain. The left hemisphere of the brain is involved in verbal, analytical and logic related activities, while the right side performs more intuitive, creative and holistic thinking tasks. Visualizing or meditating upon a yantra has been shown to bring about greater balance in the left side and right side brain activities.

One of the most powerful, auspicious and important yantras in the Tantra tradition is the Sri Chakra Yantra. Tantric texts state that worship of any deity can be undertaken in the the Sri Chakra as it is the foundation of all yantras. Adi Shankaracharya was a great believer in the power of the Sri Chakra and he had it installed in all the temples he visited.

The Vedas state that while Shiva created 64 yantras and their corresponding mantras for the welfare of humanity, he gave the knowledge of the Sri Chakra Yantra exclusively to his wife, along with its highly secret Shodasi mantra.

The deity that Sri Chakra Yantra represents is Lalita Tripurasundari but it is not called the Lalita Chakra or Tripurasundari Chakra to denote its auspiciousness and overriding power and authority.

In the tantric tradition, all symbols have three aspects:

- The Gross aspect depicting an image of the body, face, weapons, etc., of the deity
- The Subtle form which is shown in a yantra
- The Causal form which is depicted by the mantra

Tripurasundari in her gross aspect:

Lalita Tripurasundari

The Vamakeshvara Tantra describes Tripurasundari thus:

"The Dear One, Tripura is the ultimate, primordial Shakti, the light of manifestation. She, the pile of letters of the alphabet, gave birth to the three worlds. At dissolution, She is the abode of all tattvas, still remaining Herself."

Lalita means "the playful one," reflecting the Vedic philosophy which sees all creation as a mere game or play of the divine consciousness. Tripurasundari means "beauty of the three worlds" where the three worlds can signify:

Three locations: heaven, hell and earth

Three states of being: sleeping, dreaming and waking

Three gunas: tamas, rajas and sattva

The triad of human experience: intellect, feelings and physical sensation

The goddess is seen as residing in her physical and visible form in the bindu (dot) at the centre of the yantra while permeating the entire universe at the same time.

"The **Sri Chakra Yantra**, to give it the correct name, is regarded as the Supreme Yantra. Any other yantra is but a part or fraction of the Sri Yantra; it both includes and transcends all yantras ever made, and no existing yantra **cannot** be found in the Sri Yantra. The benefits of all yantras are, therefore, found (individually and collectively) in the Sri Yantra. It is also considered to be the greatest achievement in the abstract, symbolic representation of the Divine. The Sri Yantra is traditionally held to have been divinely revealed rather than invented, a concept that is easily understood when one realizes the immense complexity of the yantra."

Rohit Arya, Symbolism of the Sri Yantra

The Sri Yantra appears deceptively simple in its construction but is one of the most complex geometrical patterns in recorded history. Many accomplished mathematicians have wondered how Hindu sages were able to draw such complicated geometric patterns without any aid, even as they struggle to achieve the same with all the resources at hand. The Sri Yantra is precisely constructed to match the proportions of the Golden Ratio.

The Golden Ratio is often called the blueprint of all of creation. We see it all around us in nature (genome, DNA, flowers, seashells), art (Da Vinci's Mona Lisa and Michelangelo's art on the ceiling of the Sistine Chapel), architecture (Egyptian pyramids, Parthenon) and branding (logo of Pepsi and Nike). Even our faces and bodies follow this Golden Ratio and our perception of beauty is actually defined by this ratio. A person is seen as attractive because his/her proportions are closer to the Golden Ratio. Our brain is hardwired to prefer objects and images that are close to this ratio.

Golden Ratio in Nature

Golden Ratio in Egyptian Pyramids

Golden Ratio in Parthenon

The Sri Chakra also contains several similarities with the Flower of Life which is seen as a blueprint for the creation of sound, matter and consciousness. This pattern is seen repeated throughout nature. In the image below, we can see how a human embryo replicates the pattern of the Flower of Life.

Human embryo replicating the pattern of the Flower of Life

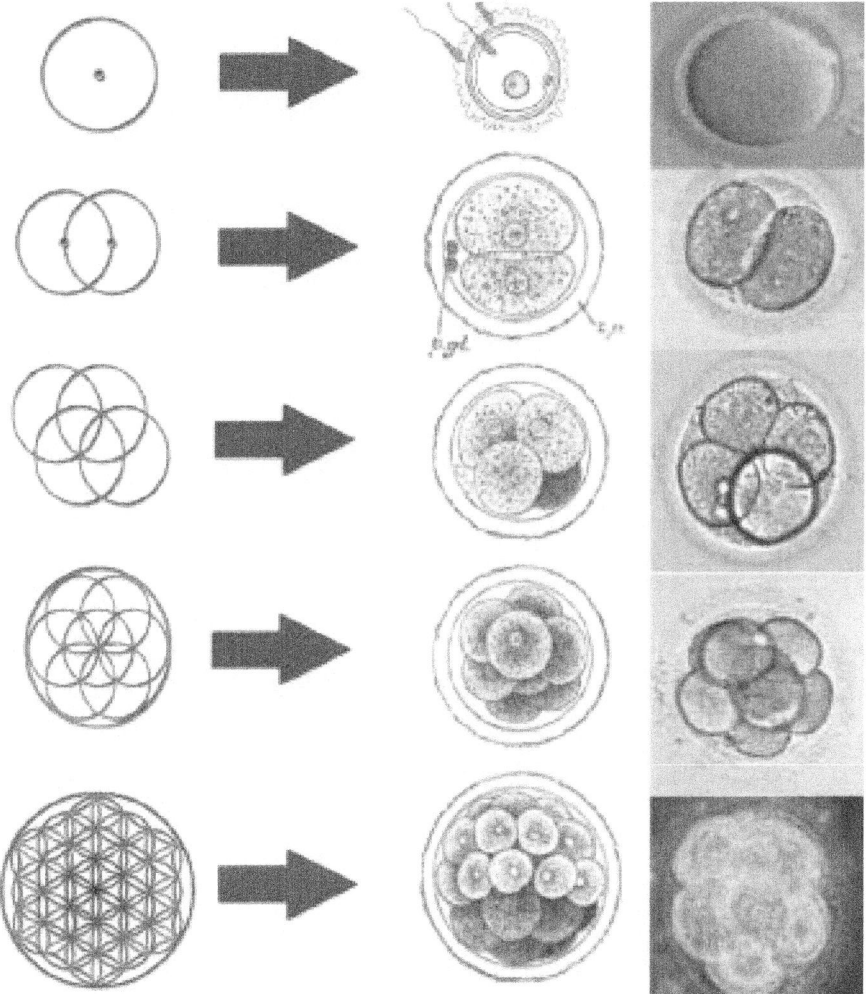

Here we can see how it is reflected in the Sri Chakra.

TONOSCOPE IMAGE OF THE SOUND OM   AN OM SHRI YANTRA (MANDALA)

The study of visible sound is called Cymatics, and it reveals some fascinating truths about our universe that go unseen by the naked eye. Sounds actually have a distinct geometry, much like crystals, flowers and nautilus shells.

When picked up by a special apparatus, such as the sand-covered plate called a tonoscope, these vibrations reveal incredible geometric shapes that are unique and beautiful.

A geometric pattern very similar to that of the Sri Chakra Yantra is created when the holy syllable Om is sounded through a tonoscope. Dr. Hans Jenny (a pioneer in the field of Cymatics) first established the correlation between sound and its vibrational patterns. It is possible that ancient Hindu sages had the knowledge to reverse-engineer the sacred sound of Om to a geometrical form. Just as the number 108 is believed to be the numeric representation of Om, the Sri Chakra Yantra is its visual representation.

A study conducted at Moscow University used an EEG machine to observe the brainwaves of test subjects who were asked to stare into a Sri Yantra. Within a few minutes of mild concentration on the geometric pattern, it was found that there was a change in the brain activities of the subjects as their brain waves slowed down considerably and reached an Alpha level, a state of mind associated with heightened intuition, greater creativity and deeper relaxation. (Source: Biology Faculty of Moscow University, October 1987)

Itagi Ravi Kumar and Jang Jungyun conducted an experiment using the Sri Yantra to see if it had any effects on the germination of green gram. Two types of the Sri Yantra - made of copper - were used. One was a two-dimensional Bhuprasthana Yantra and the other was a Mahameru Yantra. It was discovered that the samples, treated with both the yantras, showed a marked increase in percentage of germination, radical length and fresh and oven dry weight of germinated seeds when compared to the controlled sample seeds. The two-dimensional Bhuprasthana Yantra showed a more positive effect than the three-dimensional Mahameru Yantra. (Source: International Journal of Geology, Agriculture and Environmental Sciences Vol 5, Issue 2, April 2017)

R.K. Sennaya Swamy Muthukrishnan, an Indian Egyptologist travelled to the pyramids of Giza to prove that the base triangles of the great pyramids are equal in angular measurements to those found in the Sri Chakra Yantra. In his book *The Egyptian Code: The Secret Code Used by Pharaohs that Can Turn Small Businesses Into Empires*, he writes that far from being the tombs of Pharaohs, the pyramids served as a recuperation and resting place for important persons among the Egyptian elite. The bio-energy found inside a pyramid helps cure ailments and restores vitality and good health. Recent deciphering of Egyptian hieroglyphics lends credence to Muthukrishnan's theories. (Source: The Hindustan Times, Oct. 28, 1997 – Pyramidal Facts)

An award-winning American artist called Bill Witherspoon has written extensively about his experiment with a diagram of the Sri Chakra Yantra on a dry lake in Oregon. He states that after the sacred drawing was dissolved by natural causes, there were many changes recorded in the area including a noted increase in soil fertility, plant nutrients and yield. (Source: John Hopkins University – Project MUSE digital library)

The well-known American physicist Dr. Patrick Flanagan calls the Sri Yantra "the king of power diagrams," and describes its energetic effect as seventy times greater than that of a pyramid construction. (Source: Research paper by Marcus Schmieke featuring Dr. Flanagan's findings)

The Sri Chakra Yantra can be seen in three forms – plane, pyramidical and spherical. In its plane two-dimensional form, it is also called the Bhuprasthana and is typically presented as engravings on copper, silver or gold. In its three-dimensional form, it is called a Mahameru, the mythological cosmic mountain said to be at the centre of the universe.

The Mahameru in plan is same as in the plane Sri Chakra but the triangles surrounding the innermost triangle are piled on top of one another in different planes to arrive at a whole which is shaped like a pyramid. The bindu (dot) is at the topmost part of the structure. In yet another complex three-dimensional form, the Sri Chakra Yantra is presented in a spherical shape called the Kurma - as it resembles a tortoise's shell, which is phenomenally more complex in structure and construction.

Copper Sri Chakra

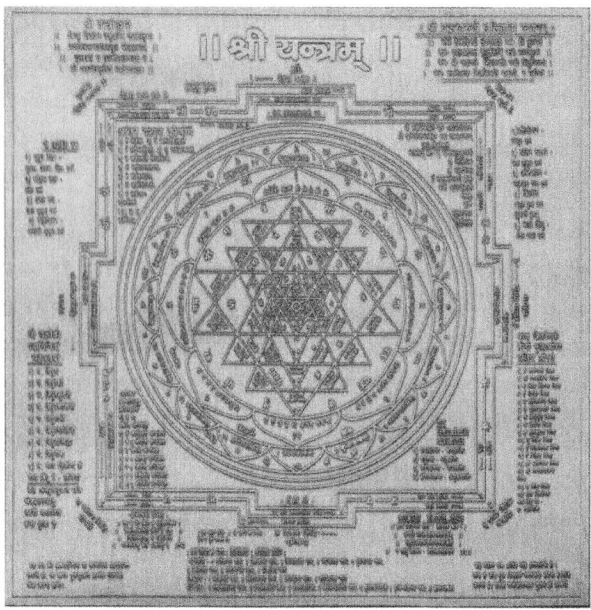

Copper Sri Chakra with Beej Mantras

Mahameru

Spherical Sri Chakra

Sri Chakra inscribed on a stone linga

Worship can be of two kinds – external worship (baahya pooja) in which the worshipper sees himself as disparate from the object of his devotion, or internal worship (antah pooja) in which the worshipper completely identifies with the object of his devotion. The Sri Chakra Yantra is a device that is used in both the forms of worship as a guide to ultimately fulfil the desires of the worshipper.

Meditation on any of the forms is acceptable and no one form is better than the other. An accurate drawing on paper will work just as well as the most intricately carved Mahameru. However, if you intend to become a serious practitioner, it is advisable to buy a two-dimensional Bhuprasthana Sri Yantra engraved on copper (as it is a good conductor of energy) after due research and checking if it indeed is an accurate representation of the sacred geometry.

3
SHAKTISM, TANTRA AND SRI VIDYA

Hindu dharma holds three concepts at the very core of its essence: Brahman (the Absolute), Vedas (sacred knowledge) and Moksha (liberation from the never-ending cycle of death and rebirth).

Brahman is the nature of truth, knowledge and infinity, according to the Taittariya Upanishad (*satyam jnanam antantam brahman*). It is above and beyond the human construct of time, space and matter. Brahman is derived from "brh" meaning "that which grows (brhati) or that which causes growth (brhmayati)." Brahman is often loosely translated as God but a deeper study suggests that it is a very specific conception of the Absolute – it transcends all dualities and classifications. The Brahman is not only the Absolute Truth (*param satya*) but also the omnipotent and animating principle of life (*chit-atman*).

The ultimate aim of a Hindu is to become one with the Brahman.

The paths to become one with the Brahman are many – knowledge, devotion, good deeds and meditation are of primary importance but there are no distinctions made between these paths as they are bound to intersect and work in combination in the due process of living.

The first path to liberation (and of particular importance to us in this book) is knowledge which is contained in the Vedas – the oldest Hindu scriptures that contain information on all aspects of life. The word Veda comes from "vid" meaning "to know" and it serves to manifest the language of Brahman to humanity. Tradition indicates that the Vedas were not composed by humans but were revealed to enlightened rishis or seers and have been passed down from generation to generation by way of oral tradition.

The Vedic knowledge is said to be "Shruti" – one which has been heard (consisting of revelations) is the unquestionable truth and can never change. Other forms of knowledge are "Smrithi" – those which are remembered (an outcome of the intellect) and can change over time.

The Vedas are not a mere collection of scriptures but a living, ever-expanding, dynamic communication between the Brahman and humanity using the subtle laws that govern the universe – sound, form and colour. Humans can utilize the knowledge contained in the Vedas to lead them to moksha, which is liberation from suffering and the endless cycle of death and rebirth. It is the return to Brahman – the realization of the self as the Absolute.

Hindu dharma clearly states that liberation is not exclusively promised to one who embraces sanyasa. It is equally possible for a householder, who aspires for material prosperity and enjoys a sensory life, to seek moksha. In both cases, the pursuit of knowledge is the starting point of the journey. A sanyasi should pursue methods that would lead him to understand his Self, while a householder should pursue learning which becomes the basis of dharma (moral duties), artha (wealth creation) and kama (sensual enjoyment).

While a sanyasi can seek his brahmavidya through renunciation, asceticism and meditation, a householder can begin his journey into the deepest point of his being through a study of the Sri Vidya.

The Sri Vidya is an ancient Shakta Tantra school of wisdom that is focused on the worship of Shakti, the feminine principle. In Hindu dharma, enlightenment is often seen as a process that takes several lifetimes. The Tantra philosophy, on the contrary, suggests that enlightenment is possible in one lifetime. Tantra does not discriminate between a householder and a renunciate in their endeavour to find liberation. The use of mantra (sacred sound) and yantra (sacred geometry) are the two key elements of Tantra.

Sri Vidya is the knowledge of the Cosmic Mother who is the queen of the three worlds (sleeping, dreaming and waking). In the tradition of the Sri Vidya, the Self is worshipped as a deity and mantras or sacred sounds are offered to the divinity that lies within us. The Sri Vidya is the embodiment of the tantric experience and all forms of tantric practices are subsumed in it.

The visual or geometric representation of the Sri Vidya is called the SRI CHAKRA.

The Brihadaranyaka Upanishad, considered to be the crown jewel among all the Upanishads, carries the famous statement "*Aham Brahmasmi* (I am Brahman or Divine Consciousness)." This pithy declaration encapsulates the entire philosophy of Sanatana Dharma, the Hindu faith. This one short statement is sufficient to disprove all the misconceptions that exist about Hinduism and the pantheon of Gods that are worshipped within its broad framework. The basic premise of Hindu dharma is that there is only one Supreme Being who is given different names, forms and assigned specific qualities. This manifestation as various divine bodies helps establish a speedier connection between humans and the divine as it reduces the Supreme Being to a more tangible, approachable and relatable entity. Throughout the history of this ancient religion, there have been many sects which have formed as an outcome of devotion to one particular form or one particular philosophy. In general, Hinduism can be categorized into four major denominations:

- Vaishnavism – worship of Vishnu
- Shaivism – worship of Shiva
- Shaktism – worship of Mother Goddess or Shakti
- Smarthaism – belief in the essential oneness of all gods; offers personal choice to the worshipper to determine his (own) God

All the four denominations are united in the common purpose that they share: to further the soul's unfoldment to its divine destiny. Several concepts such as accepting the Vedas as the ultimate authority, belief in the doctrines of karma, reincarnation, etc., are common to all.

They differ primarily in terms of the God worshipped by the particular sect as the Supreme Being and the traditions that are followed in offering worship to that God. Each of these sects has its own temples, pilgrimage centres, sacred literature and guru lineages.

Shaktas, as the practitioners of Shaktism are commonly known, conceive the Goddess as a representation of the primordial energy and source of the cosmos. Shaktism is based on the Vedas, Upanishads and Puranas that speak about the prevalence of Shaktism during different historical periods, beginning with early Vedic times, waxing and waning in its influence and gaining maximum prominence during the Epic period. Shaktism is believed to have evolved out of a rebellion against the power that Brahmins exercised in society and a desire to return to the archetypal Mother Goddess concept that existed in prehistoric times. The most important propagators of Shaktism have been the practitioners of Advaita Vedanta, including Adi Shankaracharya.

In Shaktism, the world is not approached as *maya* or illusion. It is perceived as real with all its aspects (even the ugly, gross and unholy) as divine. Shakti evolves into 36 *tattvas* or elements to create the universe. Therefore, the universe and everything it contains are a mere manifestation of Shakti. The Brihadaranyanka Upanishad contains a reference to a spider spinning its web from its mouth and moving through its own creation of concentric circles, putting forth fresh threads and pulling back others while controlling all of its creation from one single point. This image conveys the essentially Vedic thought that all existence arises out of and eventually returns to one single principle.

The human body is held sacred as it is the temple of our spiritual unfoldment.

Shaktism can be classified into Srikula or family of Lakshmi and Kalikula or the family of Kali. In both aspects, Shakti is worshipped by mantras, mudras and yantras.

One of the most well-known sub-traditions of Shaktism is Tantra, which refers to techniques, practices and rituals and involves mantra, mudra and yantra often encompass some elements of Kundalini Shakti.

One of the most popular traditions of spiritual growth in India has undoubtedly been Kundalini Shakti. Just as in most other traditions, its basic tenet is that Shakti resides within us and spiritual evolution is achieved by proper utilization of this feminine principle. In the Kundalini tradition, Shakti is seen as residing at the base of the spine at the Muladhara Chakra.

Kundalini comes from the word "serpent" as this energy is shown as lying dormant like a coiled up snake ready to wake. The goal of Kundalini is to open up all the chakras of the body, thereby allowing the ascent of Kundalini from the Muladhara to the Sahasrara, traversing through various chakras. When the energy finally reaches the top of the head, it is said to bring about enlightenment and liberation of the soul.

Tantra represents the practical aspect of Vedic traditions. It is called a *"Sadhana-shastra"* which means that it is practice-oriented as opposed to other traditions that are philosophy-oriented. Tantra accepts that the body exists with all its energies, good and bad; in the same way, the world exists with all its energies, good and bad. In this sense, tantra is seen as a body-affirming and world-affirming spiritual tradition. This is in direct contrast to the classical view, which insists on the renunciation of worldly life to attain liberation. This aspect of tantra allows householders to aspire for spiritual liberation while enjoying the sensory pleasures of life.

Pandit Rajmani Tigunait writes in the *Living Science of Tantra, Part1*:

"Tantra is an ancient yet vibrant spiritual science. It is unique in that it takes the whole person into account. Other spiritual traditions ordinarily teach that desire for worldly pleasures and spiritual aspirations are mutually exclusive, setting the stage for an endless internal struggle. Although most people are drawn to spiritual beliefs and practices, they have a natural urge to fulfil their worldly desires. With no way to reconcile these two impulses, they fall prey to guilt and self-condemnation or they become hypocritical, or both. The tantric approach to life avoids this pitfall."

There could not be a better way to explain in simple terms possibly one of the most complex, grossly misunderstood and misinterpreted terms of ancient Hindu traditions. The word tantra is sadly synonymous in the West with erotic sexual practices, while in India, it is most often labelled as occult and dark – sometimes known as "the left-hand path."

Tantra suffers from its association with macabre Aghori traditions (eating/drinking from a skull, crematorium rituals, intoxication, sexual orgies). This is so far from the truth that the Tantra tradition expounds.

The word itself is derived from *tan* (Sanskrit for "to expand" or "to spread") and *tra* (meaning instrument). Tantra literally means an instrument to expand consciousness. Some Vedic scholars also interpret that the word means "to weave," seeing the universe as a web in which everything is interconnected. As Antoaneta Gotea writes in Hridaya Yoga, Tantra philosophy can best be expressed as "Nothing exists that is not divine."

In Tantric tradition, the universe is alive and brimming with joy and bliss. All manifestations are seen as an interplay between Shiva who symbolize pure consciousness, the unchanging, unlimited masculine principle and Shakti who symbolize the activating energy, the provider and the Mother, the feminine principle. Shiva and Shakti are merely manifestations of the Brahman but it is only when Shiva and Shakti combine that creation can occur.

Tantra actually seeks to dissolve the separateness of the mundane from the spiritual. Every aspect of life is seen as a tool for spiritual growth. The body is seen as a living temple and all of its energies – positive or otherwise – are considered as tools for spiritual progress and transformation. Tantra is deeply devotional and highly ritualistic, but these rituals are a means to see and experience all of life and its energies as divine manifestations. To embody the essence of tantra that "nothing exists that is not divine," it is said that it is equal to Self-realisation.

Tantra is normally classified into three major schools, although there are many subdivisions within these:

* Kaula
* Mishra
* Samaya

Kaula Tantra practice is focussed on external rituals and processes. Mishra Tantra advocates a mixture of external rituals and processes combined with internal practices. Samaya Tantra describes a process that is completely internal, a purely yogic practice with no use for external rituals. Kaula Tantra is seen as the lower form of practice and Samaya Tantra the highest in the hierarchy of tantric practices.

The word kaula comes from the term "kula" meaning "family." This means two things: One, that this path can be practiced by those embracing family life, and two, that everything in this universe is a part of one large family, much like in the concept of Vasudaiva Kutumbakam as seen in later day Vedic texts and philosophies.

Within the Kaula Tantra, we see two types of paths - the left-handed path and the right-handed path - based on the practices that are followed. The left-hand path is known as Vamachara Marga which is a non-conformist, non-orthodox path where there is no distinction between good and bad, pure and impure, clean and unclean. Sometimes it is seen as a path that uses means which go against the norms and ethics laid down by society.

The *Panchamakara* ritual, that some Tantra practitioners follow, entails the use of taboo substances such as wine, meat, fish and sexual union. The Dakshina Marga (right-handed path) follows practices which are more conformist, focusing on the use of mantra, yantra and well-defined processes for spiritual growth. There is no wrong path in Tantra but, in modern times, the Kaula Marga has been at the receiving end of a great deal of flak as it is grossly misunderstood and misrepresented, especially by Western theologians who do not quite understand the subtleties involved in the comprehension of ancient Hindu Vedic texts.

In Tantra, Shakti (the goddess) is secret and subtle. She reveals herself to the seeker only after years of intense devotion and sadhana. Shakti, therefore, compromises the inner guiding light, the knowledge and its comprehension. Hence, Shakti is vidya.

The tantric texts speak of ten wisdom goddesses (Dasa Mahavidya) whose worship brings about health, happiness and wealth in this life and liberation from the cycle of death and rebirth thereafter.

The worship of the Dasa Mahavidya is the main path in Tantra Yoga.

Vidya means knowledge (*"vid"* means "to know"), learning, discipline and a system of thought, and when the word *Sri* is prefixed to it, it becomes knowledge which is auspicious, beneficial and conducive to prosperity. Sri is the Mother Goddess who rules over the universe *(tvam sris tvam isvari)*. She is called the mother because all living beings depend on her for the fulfilment of their destiny.

Shakti is the source of all the principles and energies of the universe. The immense diversity of the manifestations of Shakti are seen in nature – in all cosmic bodies, forces, nature, all of life's creations and human beings. These are all expressions of Shakti's vidya. Therefore, the symbols of these energies and their expressions are regarded with immense awe, wonder and reverence and known as "Maha" (great) Vidya.

Devi Puranas and Bhagavata expound the glory of Shakti as the upholder of the cosmic order. The Mahavidya tradition restricts itself to only dealing with the diverse forms of Shakti that pervade all aspects of reality. Even though Her vidya is infinite and all-pervasive, it is classified into ten Mahavidya for the purpose of simplifying the sadhana for the seeker.

The origin of Mahavidya as a group is quite unclear. Historians are of the view that Mahavidya as a cluster of ten is of comparatively recent origin, possibly between the 12th and 14th centuries. It is entirely plausible that it began as a revolt against Brahmin notions of purity and differentiation (much like Shaktism had at an earlier point in time). A cursory study of Mahavidya shows a definite urge to return to more primitive and indigenous faith as it is based more on human experience and draws from aspects of humdrum existence.

The Dasa Mahavidya

Devadutta Kali writes in the *Power of Consciousness* that "the highest spiritual truth is that reality is One. That reality, when personified as the Divine Mother, expresses itself in countless ways. The ten Mahavidya, or Wisdom Goddesses, represent distinct aspects of divinity intent on guiding the spiritual seeker toward liberation. For the devotionally-minded seeker, these forms can be approached in a spirit of reverence, love and increasing intimacy. For a knowledge-oriented seeker, these same forms can represent various states of inner awakening along the path to enlightenment."

The Mahavidya represent ten different aspects of the One Truth – the Divine Mother is adored and approached as 10 distinct cosmic personalities.

A story from the Shakta-Maha-Bhagavatha-Purana narrates the origin of the Dasa Mahavidya. Sati, daughter of Daksha Prajapathi, is madly in love with Shiva and marries him against her father's wishes. Daksha, an arrogant and angry ruler, decides to conduct a yagna to which he invites all the gods except his son-in-law Shiva. This angers Sati greatly as she sees it as an insult to her husband and makes up her mind to attend the yagna. She goes to Shiva to seek his permission but he refuses to let her go stating that even if she went, the fruit of the yagna would remain inauspicious.

Sati gets very angry with Shiva at what she perceives to be an affront to her intelligence and wishes to show him her own power. She assumes the shape of the Divine Mother in all her might. Shiva gets afraid and tries to escape her wrath. She appears in ten different forms, guarding each of the ten directions. These Goddesses jointly subdue Shiva's resistance and Sati goes on to attend the sacrificial ritual.

Each of these forms of the Divine Mother has been given a name, story, quality and their own mantras.

KALI – The first in the series of the Wisdom Goddesses represents the power of consciousness in its highest form. She is Adi Mahavidya or the primary vidya. She is beyond time and space and seen as a "Devourer of Time" and worshipped as the very essence of the Brahman.

Kali is, at once, the supreme power and ultimate reality, bringing home the fundamental tantra tenet that consciousness and the power of consciousness are both the exact same thing.

The first transcendent cosmic power takes away all darkness and fills us with the light of wisdom; hence, she is the very embodiment of Jnana Shakti. She symbolizes the power of transformation. The rest of the Mahavidyas emanate from Kali and reflect her virtues, powers and nature in varying shades.

TARA – The Goddess is variously understood as "a star" who is beautiful but perpetually self-combusting. She is seen as a guide and a protector who helps her devotees "to cross" the ocean of worldly existence. Tara symbolizes everything in the cosmos that is absolute, unquenchable hunger that propels all of life. She, therefore, symbolizes the gracious liberator.

Tara's symbolism is often related to death but, in its broadest sense as the death of the ego, she removes the mistaken notions we have of our own identities.

LALITA TRIPURA SUNDARI – She is one who is "the most beautiful in the three worlds." The three worlds could variously be described as:

1. The three states of consciousness – sleeping, waking and dreaming

2. The three aspects of humanity – the physical body, the causal body and the astral body

3. The three aspects of the universe – matter, energy and thought

4. The three aspects of energy – Iccha Shakti (the energy of will), jnanashakti (the energy of knowledge) and kriyashakti (the energy of action)

Tripurasundari is also known as Lalita or the one who plays. The Hindu spiritual tradition asserts that the whole of creation is nothing more than a beautiful, charming game or play of the Divine Mother.

Tripurasundari is shown with four arms holding five arrows of flowers, a goad, a noose and a sugarcane bow.

The five arrows symbolize our five senses; the goad represents repulsion; the noose stands for attachment; the sugarcane bow is an analogy for the mind.

She symbolizes our need to purify our awareness and cleanse the mind of unworthy thought(s). She also symbolizes wealth.

Lalita Tripurasundari has three manifestations: Sthula or descriptive as in an image; Sukshma or subtle as in a mantra; para or transcendent as in a yantra. The yantra associated with this form of Devi is the Sri Chakra Yantra which is the subject of study of this book.

For our study, Tripurasundari will be the main focus as she is also known as the Adi Mahavidya or the primordial Wisdom Goddess who resides in the Sri Chakra.

BHUVANESHWARI – The Goddess is known as World Mother. "Bhuvana" means "this living world" and "isvari" means "ruler." She embodies all the characteristics of the cosmos. She is identified with the manifest world and all that we experience within it. The entire universe is said to be her body and all the beings are ornaments of her infinite being. She carries all the worlds as a flowering of her own Self-nature.

The symbolism of Bhuvaneshwari, who is all pervasive and completely identifies with the universe, is an invitation for us to cultivate an attitude of universality. She represents the power of openness and infinite expansion, of equanimity in spirit and profound peace that contains in it all things that cannot be disturbed.

BHAIRAVI – The fierce and terrifying aspect of Devi, also called Shubhamkari, is believed as a good mother to good people and terrible to the bad ones. She evokes terror and fear and is seen seated on a headless corpse in a cremation ground with four arms. In one hand she's holding a sword of knowledge and in another a demon's head while two arms are shown in mudras - one abhayamudra which teaches us to have no fear and the other varadamudra that grants all boons.

Bhairavi symbolizes the maternal instinct to protect offspring. She destroys ignorance and helps us overcome the negative forces that exist within ourselves and at the same time manifest our material desires.

CHINAMMASTA – She is known as the self-decapitated Goddess. The Panchatantra Grantha tells the story of Parvati who once goes to bathe in the Mandakini river with her two close friends. As the day progresses, the friends get hungry and ask Parvathi for food. She keeps putting them off until their demands grow incessant. At one point, she laughingly cuts off her head using her fingernail and blood spurts out in three directions. The two friends drink in the blood from two founts, while Parvati drinks from the third.

The severed head symbolize liberation. However, the most symbolic message of this form of the Goddess is that we all possess rare courage needed to make the ultimate sacrifice.

The blood spurting from her neck represents prana (cosmic life force) which sustains her own life as well as that of all other beings in the universe.

Chinnamasta can also be interpreted as an awakening of the kundalini in each one of us as we rid ourselves of our mistaken identities and overcome limitations that hinder our spiritual progress.

DHUMAVATI – She is the one made of smoke - that which is dark, polluting and conceals the truth – the worst facets of humanity. This transcendent power shows us that a dark side of life is very much a reality that we all have to confront. This form of the Divine Consciousness is associated with poverty, hunger, thirst and anger - all the aspects of living which everyone wishes to avoid.

Dhumavati stands for the corrosive power of time that robs us of all that is valuable to us – loved ones, beauty, vigour, vitality. The lesson from Dhumavati is to understand the transient nature of all the experiences. She is a great teacher who reveals the ultimate knowledge of the universe and teaches us to cultivate a sense of detachment from our senses.

BAGALAMUKHI – She is the one who paralyzes enemies. This form of Devi smashes misconceptions and delusions (enemies of spiritual growth). Tantra Shastra describes her as sitting on a golden throne in the middle of an ocean. Though generally depicted as a goddess with a human head, she is also shown with the head of a crane in some iconography.

She ceases all motion at the appropriate time and silences the mind. She is praised as the giver of siddhi and riddhi (supernatural and magical powers) to her devotees who seek her with sadhana.

MATANGI – The tantric form of Goddess Saraswathi is another ferocious aspect of Devi. The Dhyana mantra of Brhat Tantrasastra describes Matangi as seated on a corpse, wearing red garments and red jewellery, carrying a skull and a sword in her two hands. Worship of Matangi is said to give her devotees the ability to face the forbidden, transcend pollution of the senses and lead them to gain supernatural powers for attaining worldly goals and ultimately salvation. Meditation on Matangi is prescribed especially to gain control over enemies, attract people and acquire mastery over the arts.

KAMALA – The Lotus Goddess, called the "Tantric Lakshmi," is a form that holds the promise of wealth, prosperity and well-being. She sits holding a lotus with two hands and bestowing blessings with the other two. The lotus is a recurrent symbol of the manifest universe in the Hindu tradition. It grows out of the murky water but brings forth beauty and fragrance. In the same way, it is possible for us humans, with our restricted material body, amidst all the pollution of life, to rise above and emerge as Divine Consciousness.

Kamala symbolize the unfolding of inner consciousness much like the petals of a lotus. She is worshipped in the hope of bringing material wealth. The lesson from Kamala is to see beauty in everything around us and to understand that true wealth is only achieved when it is selflessly shared with others.

Undoubtedly, the Mahavidya, as a group with its individual deities, depicts some of the most unusual, fierce, strange and vivid gods ever portrayed in any major world religion or culture. The forms are radically different from the benign and beautiful gods worshipped in the "cultured" society. They challenge accepted norms of social order with their outlandish behaviour, grotesque bodies, ugly faces and bizarre habits. These outrageous manifestations are meant to shock us and compel us to look beyond our comfort zones. The disturbing and distressing aspects force us to look deeper into our own selves to identify our shortcomings and show us for what we are, not what we are meant to be.

By rejecting and subverting conventionally accepted norms, the Mahavidya seeks to expand awareness to liberate the mind from inhibitions and prejudices.

An interesting aspect of the Mahavidya is that even though they are all about the power of the feminine principle, the deities are not shown as wives (although spouses are named in a few forms) or as mothers.

It is natural to wonder about the reason why our ancient seers divided all the great knowledge into ten diverse aspects. Vedic scholars have indicated that it was an effort to drive home certain important points:

1. The Divine Mother is Absolute, ineffable and immutable and is beyond time and space.
2. In the act of creation, she subjects herself to constraints of time and space.

    Time is an aspect of prakruthi (Nature) and one of the 36 tattvas or principles of creation. However, as a concept, it is a creation of our intellect based on our sensory perception. It is a part of "Maya" or illusory state in which we all exist. For the Divine Consciousness, there is no division of time – there is only the present moment, a continuous and undivided state of existence.

    Space is vast and beyond our comprehension. It is infinite, without a beginning or an end. To simplify matters, we divide it into ten cardinal directions – East, West, North, South, South-east, South-west, North-east, North-west, above and below.

3. Knowledge is one but is understood in ten different ways based on our five sense organs and five organs of action – skin, eye, ear, nose, tongue, mouth, foot, hand, anus and genitalia.

4. Truth is one but we perceive it in various facets, shapes, forms and meanings.

S. Shankaranarayanan says in his article on "The Ten Great Cosmic Powers":

"Each has a particular Cosmic function and leads to a special realization of the One Reality. The might of Kali, the sound-force of Tara, the beauty and bliss of Sundari, the vast vision of Bhuvaneshwari, the effulgent charm of Bhairavi, the striking force of Chinnamasta, the silent inertness of Dhumavati, the paralyzing power of Bhagalamukhi, the expressive play of Matangi and the concord and harmony of Kamala are the various characteristics, the distinct manifestations of the Supreme Consciousness that have made this creation possible. The Tantra says that the Supreme can be realized at these various points."

Each one of the Mahavidya holds individual significance as Brahmavidya and together as a group they contain all the wisdom of the universe – of past, present and the future and all the potential that ever existed or will exist. A true learner, who seeks with devotion, will be guided and inspired to find the spiritual strength and capability lying dormant within him to have his dreams manifested through a study of these great systems of knowledge.

The forms of Kali and Tara are considered the only two Mahavidya. Bhairavi, Bhuvaneshwari and Chinnamasta are called Vidya; Dhumavathi, Bagalamukhi, Matangi and Kamala are called Siddhi Vidya; Tripurasundari is called Sri Vidya.

In the Rig Veda, Sri Vidya is found as Sri Sukta. While in the Brahmanda Purana there is a comprehensive description of Sri Vidya, its method and philosophy. Saundarya Lahiri, a hymn consisting of one hundred verses expounding the virtues of Lalitha Tripurasundari, is considered the most beautiful and profound explanation of Sri Vidya.

The Formation of the Sri Chakra Yantra

54 | Sri Chakra Yantra

Two exact Śri Yantras

The pattern of the Sri Yantra is a matrix of nine intersecting triangles. Five of these triangles that have their apex facing downward represent five forms of feminine energy Shakti. The four triangles with their apex facing upward are known as Shiva trikonas representing the male aspect of Shiva.

The triangle or trikona enclosure after the bindu is described as the primary triangle (mula-trikona) and is regarded as the Mother Goddess. This triangle is looked upon as pure sattva, the light of consciousness in its pristine, unfettered, unconditioned and unevolved state.

It represents the iconic form of Mother Goddess as the conjoint manifestation of three powers (inclination, knowledge and activity) associated with all phenomenal details, and the three gunas (sattva, rajas and tamas) responsible for all creation. The three angles or corners represent the dimensions of all existence (tri-khanda) - fire (Agni), sun (Surya) and moon (Chandra) - and the dimensions of the individuality - self (atma), the inner self (antar atma) and the transcendental self (paramatma). The trikona also suggest the three processes of existence - creation (srishti), preservation (sthiti) and withdrawal (samhara).

(Taken from *Srividya and Sri Chakra* by 'Lalitanandanadha' Lalita Prasad Jammulamadaka)

The intersection of these nine triangles creates 43 triangles.

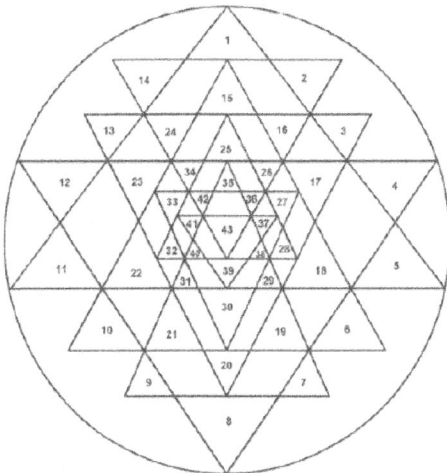

The intersection of two lines is called a sandhi and it is significant as it represents the union of Shiva and Shakti. There are 24 such sandhis.

The intersection of three lines is called a marma sthana and implies an explicit harmony between Shiva and Shakti. In the human body, marma is known as the seat of life energy or jiva shakti. There are 18 such marma sthanas.

The 43 triangles are arranged in nine enclosures that are known as the navavaranas or nine chakras ("chakra" in Sanskrit stands for "a spinning vortex").

We can approach the Sri Yantra as a spiritual pilgrimage. We need to travel from the outer walls to the innermost part of the yantra through different levels of obstacles that come in our path. The nine avaranas represent the clouding of our consciousness that needs to be cleared, and as we traverse each level, we find ourselves getting closer to understanding of the non-duality. Our thoughts get refined on the inward journey as we let go of our mistaken identities, fears and desires. Our minds are purified as we withdraw from the illusion of reality and arrive at a point (the bindu) where we become one with the Divine Consciousness.

The nine avaranas described below are according to the Dakshinamurty tradition, starting from the outermost enclosure and leading towards the bindu. This is said to be in the order of absorption (*samhara krama*).

■	**9th Avarana:** Bhupura
◠	**8th Avarana:** Shodashi Dala Padma (16 petalled lotus)
⌒	**7th Avarana:** Asta Dala Padma (8 petalled lotus)
▲	**6th Avarana:** Chaturdasha (14 triangles)
▲	**5th Avarana:** Bahirdasha (10 triangles)
▲	**4th Avarana:** Antardasha (10 inner triangles)
▲	**3rd Avarana:** Ashtakona (8 triangles)
▼	**2nd Avarana:** Trikona (triangle)
○	**1st Avarana:** Bindu (dot)

Avarana means a curtain of "not knowing" that clouds our consciousness. This, along with Mala (mental and physical impurity) and Vikshepa (internal and external disturbances that constantly torment us), make up the three main obstacles to a person's search for the truth and hinder him from recognizing that he is no different from the Divine Consciousness.

There is a very interesting story in the puranas that explains Avarana. A lion cub is left abandoned in a forest upon his mother's death and he has to fend for himself to stay alive. He sees a group of goats grazing nearby. He stays with them as they offer him companionship and solace. Soon, he learns all the habits of the goats and finds no reason to believe that he is any different from them.

One day, after many years, a lion, in search of prey, attacks the group and the lion who thinks of himself as a goat. They, along with the lion cub, flee to save their lives. Seeing this, the older lion calls upon the cub and asks him why he is afraid as he is not a goat. The younger lion is surprised as he has no idea that he is anything but a goat. The older lion takes him to the river to show him his reflection in the water. The younger lion then realizes his true self.

In the same way, we are all bound to progress in our paths unaware of our mistaken identities about ourselves and only a realization of our true nature can free us and put us back on the path in a new light.

The navavaranas:

1. Bhupura Trayam – the square field
2. Shodasa Dala Padma – the 16 petalled lotus
3. Ashta Dala Padma - the 8 petalled lotus
4. Chatur Dasara- the 14 intersecting triangles
5. Bahir Dasara - the 10 outward triangles
6. Antar Dasara - the 10 inward triangles
7. Ashta Kona - the 8 triangles
8. The Kamakala Trikona - the primary triangle

9. The space between the Bindu and the Trikona

Avaranas 2 to 6 constitute the Shakti aspect

Avaranas 7 to 9 constitute the Shiva aspect

The Bindu is the union of Shiva and Shakti

First Avarana

The outer part of the Sri Yantra is called the Bhupura or 4-sided enclosed wall and is seen as the first avarana. In Vedic texts, the earth is depicted as a square and the tantra designs of mandalas always contain a protective outer wall – much like a fort.

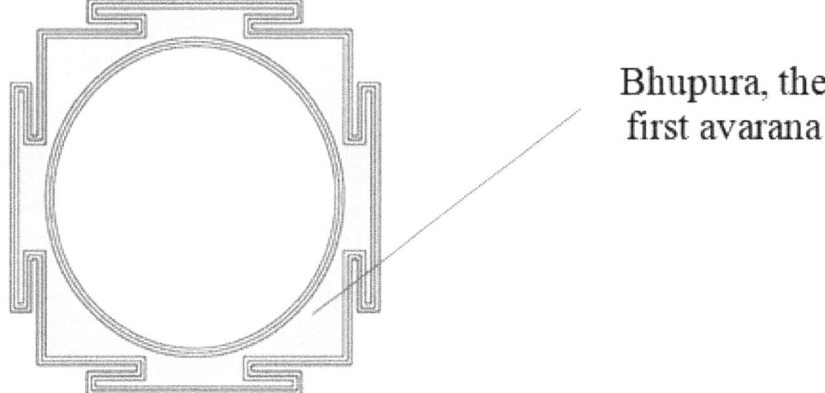

Bhupura, the first avarana

The Bhupura consists of three lines making up a square. The outermost square represents mundane emotions such as anger, fear and worldly desires. These emotions need to be overcome as a pilgrim begins his journey. This square also stands for the eight siddhis or yogic powers which are needed for self-protection on the inward journey. The eight siddhis can be obtained once we have control over our minds and the elements.

The middle line stands for mother-like divinities known as Mathrika who rule over our emotions. They include greed, stubbornness, longing, anger, etc.

The inner line represents ten feminine deities known as Mudra devatha. These can be approached in three ways:

Sthula (gross) – mudras or hand gestures

Sukshma (subtle) – mantras or sound energy

Para (transcendent) – intuition

The gateways or entry points to the yantra can be seen as the T shapes found in 4 directions.

This brings us to the three concentric circles known as Trivritta. The circles represent the principle of eternity - no beginning, no end, being perfectly symmetrical and at all points equidistant from the centre.

These are not a part of the Avaranas but exist to girdle or provide a net for the inner pattern.

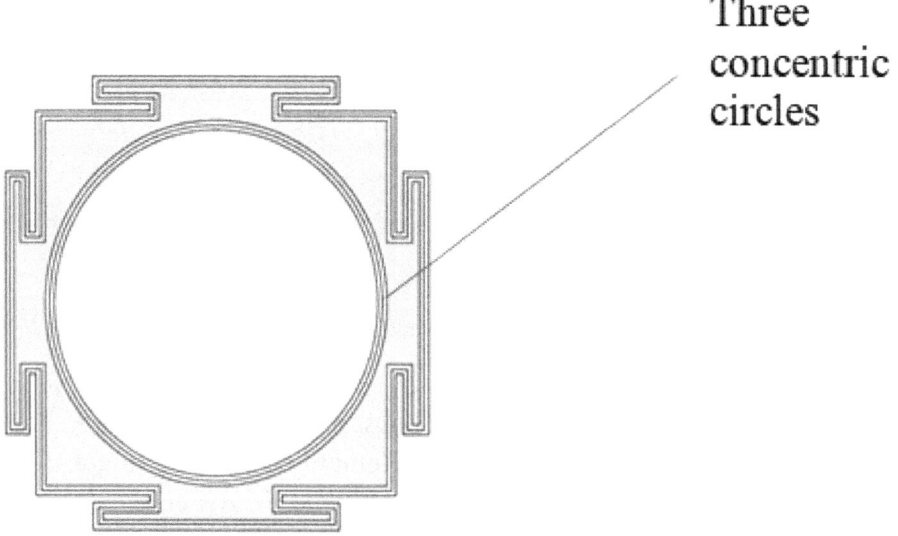

Three concentric circles

The three circles are said to variously represent:

Three aspects of time: past, present and future

Three states of being: waking, sleeping and dreaming

Three levels of experience: attainment, obstruction and power

Second Avarana

Inside the first circle are 16 outward opening lotus petals. Lotus petals are extensively used in Indian iconography and symbolism.

The lotus is very responsive to sunlight; it blossoms at sunrise and closes at sunset. In the context of the Sri Yantra, the unfolded petals signifie an expansion of consciousness and blooming of our inherent potential.

All the centres of consciousness in the subtle body are described as lotuses in Hindu texts for this reason.

This first avarana/circle is called Sarva asha paripuraka chakra (the fulfilment of all desires and hopes). The 16 petals depict

5 organs of perception

5 organs of action

5 elements

+

Mind

This avarana allows the practitioner to fulfil all his desires so that he can then choose to renounce them having enjoyed all worldly pleasures.

At this point, all discontentment is removed and the mind is now in control and strengthened to encounter other hurdles in the journey.

Third Avarana

The third avarana is called Sarva samkshobana chakra (the agitator of all). This is an eight petalled lotus which represents pleasures we derive through our organs. It has a particular reference to our erotic urges. Each petal governs a specific activity: speech, grasping, motion, excretion, enjoyment, revulsion, attraction and equanimity

Fourth Avarana

Within the inner lotus lies the first set of fourteen interlocked triangles which form the fourth avarana called Sarva sowbhagya dayaka (bestower of all prosperity).

The fourteen outward triangles are said to correspond to the same number of nadis found in the human body. Nadis are the energy channels prana (life force) moves through. These channels permeate the entire subtle body. According to classical yoga texts, there are 72,000 nadis in the human body.

The fourteen triangles represent the following traits: agitation, pursuit, attraction, delight, delusion, immobility, release, control, pleasure, intoxication, accomplishment of desire, luxury, mantra and the destruction of duality.

The advent of inner realization begins in this avarana as the practitioner begins to withdraw himself from all sensory delights and starts to become aware that he is not different from the Divine Consciousness.

Fifth Avarana

Then we arrive at the fifth avarana - ten triangles which constitute the Sarvartha Sadhaka (Accomplisher of all objects). These triangles represent deities that preside over the ten vital forces in the body. These forces can be divided into Prana Panchaka and Naga Panchaka. The Prana Panchaka vayus include:

- Prana
- Apana
- Vyana
- Udana
- Samana

These vayus or energies are involuntary actions such as:

- Respiration
- Circulation
- Digestion
- Assimilation
- Voice

The Naga Panchaka controls actions such as belching, yawning, batting of eyelids and other sounds that are produced within the body.

Sixth Avarana

From the ten-sided outer figure, we journey further into the sixth avarana - the ten-sided inner figure that make up the Sarva Rakshakara avarana (Protector of all). The ten triangles represent Vanyaha or ten vital fires necessary to stay alive.

* Purgation
* Digestion
* Absorption
* Burning
* Secretion of enzymes
* Acidification
* Excretion
* Assimilation
* Creation of lustre
* Fire of pessimism and frustration

Seventh Avarana

We now move inward to the seventh avarana - an eight-cornered avarana called Sarva roga hara (the remover of all illnesses). The eight triangles in this avarana are presided over by deities that control speech. This means that all Sanskrit alphabets are covered in this. They also rule over -

1. The inherent contradictions (dwandha) in life - heat (fire) and cold (water), sorrow and joy, etc.
2. Desire
3. The three gunas - rajas, tamas and sattva

This avarana symbolize the power to remove the most basic of diseases and to reveal our attachment with the fleeting existence of our being.

Eighth Avarana

We arrive at the eighth avarana - Kama kala or the primary triangle. With its apex facing downward, it signifies feminine energy. This avarana is known as Sarva siddhi prada (one that bestows all accomplishments). This triangle is the only one in the pattern to have no intersections; it stands independent. The three corners of the triangle represent various aspects of the universe:

* Creation, Preservation and Dissolution
* Will (iccha), knowledge(jnana) and activity (kriya)

Ninth Avarana

We have finally arrived at the most important aspect of the Sri Yantra– the bindu, the dimensionless point at the core. This avarana is called Sarvananda maya (the supremely blissful). The bindu, independent of the intersecting triangles, can be compared to the garba gudi (sanctum sanctorum) of a temple. It is here the Divinity resides. Tantra texts say the bindu, in reality, is the Sri Chakra and everything else beyond it is merely manifestation of its various aspects.

The bindu represents five principles (pancha kriya) of the cosmos:

1. Emanation
2. Projection of creation
3. Preservation of the created universe
4. Withdrawal of the creative energies in cosmic dissolution
5. Retention of the withdrawn energy of the universe for the next cycle of creation

The bindu stands for absolute harmony (Samarasa – the most sought after component of Tantra) between Shiva and Shakti. In other words, the bindu is Brahman itself. When with the power of will (iccha Shakti), the bindu expands into a triangle as an apparent differentiation takes place between Shiva and Shakti.

Having progressed through the various veils of consciousness, we can now delineate what the nine enclosures represent.

1. The first avarana deals with emotions and achievements

2. The second avarana deals with 5 pranas, 5 sense organs, 5 organs of action and the mind (this is described in detail in the next chapter – Sri Chakra and the human Body).

3. The third avarana deals with the psychosocial properties common in all humans as we go about our lives – expression of thoughts, apprehensions of the mind (especially of the future), movement, lust, attention to certain things, rejection of certain things, elimination and detachment.

4. The fourth avarana deals with mental agitation, chasing away evil thoughts, physical attraction, happiness, delusion, obstruction in the path of self-realization, releasing obstructions, surrender, experiencing bliss and accomplishing all desires (including material wealth and spiritual satisfaction) and finally dispelling all types of dualities.

5. The fifth avarana deals with the ten different types of prana (vital life forces) while removing all sorrows and offering fulfilment of every type of desire.

6. The sixth avarana deals with acquiring the necessary knowledge, spiritual energy and gaining mastery, leading to self-realization. At this stage, the practitioner seeks to be free from all diseases and is actively involved in removing all traces of karmic afflictions as the mind reaches a state of bliss.

7. The seventh avarana deals with the five types of prana, five elements and the four antahkarana (manas, buddhi, cittam and ahaṃkāra or ego).

8. The eighth avarana deals with completely freeing the mind of all afflictions and dissolving the human traits such as attachment, sensory involvement, ego and desire. The mind is freed from maya to a large extent.

9. The ninth avarana deals with the union of Shiva and Shakti, thereby leading the practitioner to a state of ultimate bliss and peace. Every form of duality is removed as all the differences between the knower, the object of knowing and the process of knowing disappear and all of them come together in absolute harmony.

This absolute harmony is depicted in the patterns and layout of the Sri Chakra. As a representation of the microcosm and the macrocosm being one and the same, the yantra provides a model for individual transformation. The practitioner arrives at the realizations that (1) his body is the Sri Chakra, (2) if his body is the residence of the Divine Consciousness, then he himself is the Divine Consciousness and (3) all the powers, energies and manifestations are but mere reflections of pure awareness and consciousness.

4
SRI CHAKRA AND THE HUMAN BODY

The human body is seen as a microcosm of the universe and the Sri Chakra Yantra is said to be a geometric representation of the cosmos. So, it stands to reason that there has to be a correlation between the human body and the formation of the Sri Chakra. We will explore this aspect in the chapter.

In Hindu tradition, a living being is made up of mind, body and spirit. The Sharira Tatva (Doctrine of Three Bodies) describes that the human body consists of 3 aspects and 5 sheaths. The three aspects arise from the Brahman (Divine Consciousness) and are a result of ignorance or avidya.

Sthula Sharira or the gross physical body

Sukshma Sharira or the subtle body

Karana Sharira or the causal body

The Sthula Sharira is the gross physical body through which life or jiva is experienced. The main features of this body include birth, ageing and death. It is related to the waking state.

The Sukshma Sharira is the subtle body that houses the mind and vital energies (prana). The subtle body is said to be composed of the five elements (air, fire, water, earth and space) and made up of the five sense organs (ear, eye, nose, tongue and skin), five organs of action (hand, foot, mouth, anus and genitalia) and the five-fold vital breath (respiration, elimination, circulation, digestion and actions such as sneezing, crying, etc.) along with Manas (mind) and Buddhi (intellect).

The dream state is the distinct state of this Sharira.

The Karana Sharira is the causal body that merely contains the seed of the Sthula and Sukshma Sharira and it has no other function of its own. It is the most complex of the three bodies and is thought to be the portal to enter higher consciousness. It is identified with the deep sleeping state.

The gross body ceases to exist when death occurs and it then becomes one with the nature. The subtle body disintegrates when it is time to take a new birth, allowing us to develop a new personality in the new life. The causal body incarnates again and again with each rebirth and carries the imprints of the karmas of our previous lives (samskaras) and disintegrate only at the time of moksha or liberation.

Each body has a dimension or a layer. In Vedanta, this layer is called a sheath or a kosha as it separates the body from the Atman (soul). Each sheath is made up of increasingly finer shades of energy beginning from the outermost layer of the skin to the innermost spiritual core of our being.

There are 5 such sheaths:

1. Annamaya Kosha
2. Pranamaya Kosha
3. Manomaya Kosha
4. Vignanamaya Kosha
5. Anandamaya Kosha

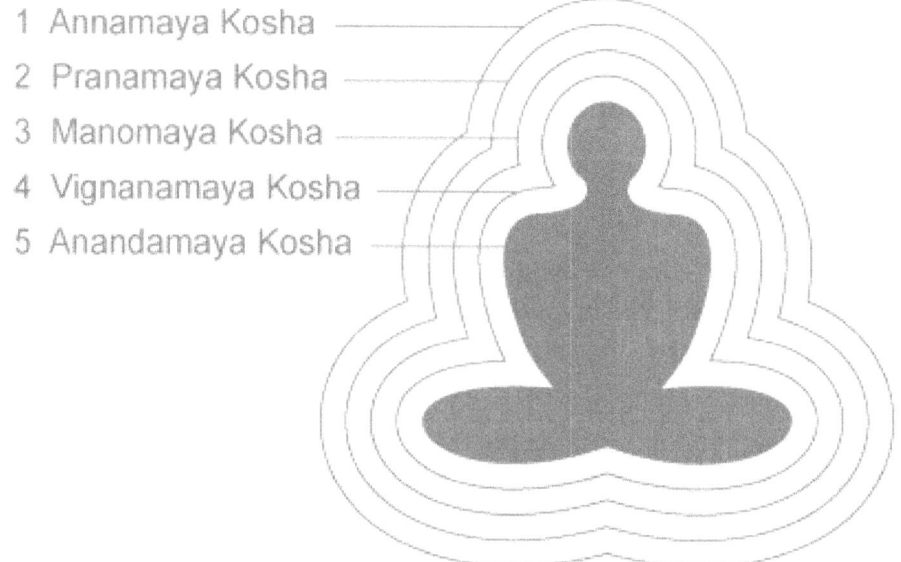

Annamaya Kosha

This is the outermost layer or the physical or food sheath which includes in it skin, connective tissue, fat, muscle and bone. "Anna" comes from "food" which our bodies take from earth and eventually turn into food for other creatures. This layer is possibly the one we find ourselves thinking about most of the time to pursue physical gratification and enjoyment.

Pranamaya Kosha

This is the sheath of subtle, vital energy (prana) and includes in it the movement of bodily fluids such as blood circulation, lymph and cerebral fluids and the circulation of breath through the respiratory system. We cannot see energy but can certainly feel it in our bodies. This layer is involved in our intuitions and impulses and therefore can be said to control our bodily and spirit rhythm.

Manomaya Kosha

This is the sheath of the mind and includes in it our emotions, feelings and workings of the nervous system. It involves the processing of inputs through our five senses and responding to them reflexively without conscious application of focus. Our thoughts, fantasies and daydreams all constitute this kosha as they are all methods of making sense of the outside world. On the most basic level, we are talking about perceptions, images and emotions, but at a deeper level resides our prejudices, preconceived notions and beliefs that we absorb over a lifetime.

Vignanamaya Kosha

This is the sheath of wisdom or the psyche. Sensory perceptions coming from the Manomaya Kosha are processed here and meaning is imbued into them with awareness, insight and consciousness. It is here that we make choices about every aspect of living/our lives based on our experiences so far. This sheath can be seen as the one housing our intelligence as we engage in activities that help us gather wisdom by way of conscious awareness.

Anandamaya Kosha

This is the sheath of bliss as we move from conscious awareness to pure bliss which includes in it our unconscious mind, samskaras (impressions left behind by every life experience) and our individual consciousness called Chitta. In this sheath, there is nothing but sheer joy and utter contentment. There are no mortal fears or base emotions such as anger, jealousy and insecurities. Among the five sheaths, the Anandamaya Kosha reflects the Divine Consciousness and its state of satchidananda (eternal bliss).

The fact that each of the koshas is suffixed with the word "maya" (illusion) points to their illusory nature. They may appear to separate us from the Divine Consciousness but that is merely illusory. This is an indication the Vedic texts have left for us that even though we point out all these differences, we are not separate from the Divine.

To understand the development of the process by which energy condenses from the unmanifest to the gross physical form of the human body, we can think of the Anandamaya Kosha as ether or space, Vijnanamaya Kosha as air, Manonmaya Kosha as steam, Pranamaya Kosha as water and Annamaya Kosha as ice. Just as it is more difficult to give shape to ice than to water, (as ice is solid and water as a liquid takes on the shape of its container more easily than ice) the more ephemeral the various sheaths become as we move towards the higher realms.

All across Vedic literature, it is reiterated that the human body is a microcosm of the universe. Whatever exists in the universe is seen in the human body and vice versa. The human body is believed to be made up of two parts – one from the top of the head till the end of the spine and the other from the end of the spine to the feet. Therefore, the spine is the axis on which the body rests just as the Meru is the axis of the universe. It is for this reason that the spine is called Merudanda.

Sutras in the Bhavanopanishad (*"bhavana"* means "imagination or concept formation in the mind") help us contemplate our body within the Sri Chakra. The nine triangles (intersection of 5 shakti and 4 shiva triangles) are seen as the nine apertures (*navarandha*). They are:

Eyes – 2 openings

Ears – 2 openings

Nostrils – 2 openings

Mouth – 1 opening

Organ of procreation – 1 opening

Organ of excretion – 1 opening

The inward journey of a practitioner begins with the feet and moves upward till it reaches a point above the crown of the head. The nine avaranas, therefore, have their own corresponding body parts.

The nine avaranas and their correspondence to the parts of the body

Bhupura	First square – feet
	Middle square – knees
	Inner square – thighs
Three concentric circles	Middle portion of the body
Shodasi Dala Padma	From the genital area till below the navel
Ashta Dala Padma	The navel
Chaturdasha	The abdominal region
Bahir dasha	The neck
Antar dasha	Region between the eyebrows
Ashtakona	Forehead
Trikona	Top of the head
Bindu	Above the crown

The Chakras in the Human Body

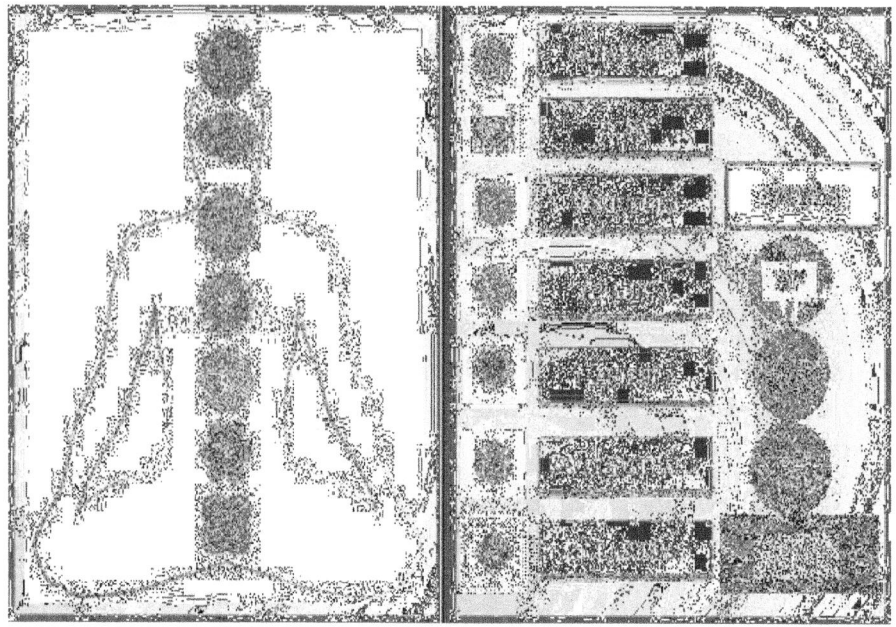

Chakra is a Sanskrit word that translates to a spinning disk or vortex. The three main nadis (energy channels) – Ida, Pingala and Sushumna – run along the spinal column in a curved path and criss-cross at several points. These points of intersection are strong energy centres known as chakras. A chakra, therefore, acts as a centre of activity that receives, assimilates and expresses prana.

In Ayurveda, it is believed that the human body in its subtle form (Sukshma Sharira) has 21 chakras but 7 of them are the most important which serve as the conduits of prana or life energy. The seven chakras lie between the base of the spine and the top of the crown.

Each chakra has a specific purpose and area of influence. Physically, the chakras correlate to specific locations, tissues and glands and serve a specific function on a physical, mental/emotional and spiritual level.

Chakras and their corresponding body parts and glands

Chakra	Body Part	Gland
Muladhara	Kidney, spine	Reproductive
Swadhisthana	Bladder, prostate, gall bladder, spleen, bowels	Adrenal
Manipuraka	Intestines, pancreas, liver, stomach, upper spine	Pancreas
Anahata	Heart and lungs	Thymus
Vishuddha	Bronchial tubes, vocal cords, respiratory system, esophagus, mouth and tongue	Thyroid
Ajna	Eyes	Pituitary
Sahasrara	Spinal cord and brain stem	Pineal

The chakras are subtle in nature and hence are not visible or tangible to the regular five senses. In order to make the chakras more perceptible and easy to understand, each chakra is associated with a colour, symbol, sound and element. Each chakra is depicted as a lotus flower with a specific number of petals to represent the number of nadis leading to and from that particular chakra.

Colours and sounds associated with chakras

Chakra	Colour	Sound
Muladhara	Red	Lam
Swadhisthana	Orange	Vam
Manipuraka	Yellow	Ram
Anahata	Green	Yam
Vishuddha	Light blue	Ham
Ajna	Indigo blue	Om
Sahasrara	Purple	Om

Since all of nature is in a state of constant flux, it is important that the 7 chakras are active and in a constant state of motion. A block in one of the chakras will hamper the flow of prana, thereby resulting in stagnation, ill health and spiritual disconnectedness.

The nine avaranas are recognized as chakras lying along the central channel or the Sushumna nadi. Commonly understood, there are seven chakras. But here we see the inclusion of two more chakras - the Manas-chakra and the Soma-chakra. These are located just above the Ajna chakra and lie one above the other. There is a deep connection between the moon and the mind. If the mind chakra is balanced and open, it allows the Kundalini to rise to the Sahasraha without obstacle. These two chakras are very important in the journey of spiritual development and ascent beyond the physical.

The Navavarana and their corresponding chakras

Bhupura	Muladhara
Shodasa Dala Padma	Swadisthana
Ashta Dala Padma	Manipuraka
Chaturdasha	Anahata
Bahir Dasha	Vishuddha
Antar dasha	Ajna
Ashtakona	Manas-chakra
Trikona	Soma-chakra
Bindu	Sahasrara

The Sri Chakra also represents a diagram of the cycle of time (Kaalachakra). The breath is intricately linked with the concept of time. Breathing is influenced by the five elements present in the body and vice versa. It is for this reason that the focus is on Pranayama in all yogic and meditative literatures.

On an average, an adult human being takes 360 breaths in a unit of time called nadika where one nadika is equal to about 24 minutes. One day consists of 60 nadikas. In a day, therefore, we breathe 21,600 times.

This is called the nadi chakra or the organization of breaths in the body. The texts further describe that breath is distributed among the various chakras which are mentioned below:

Chakra	No. of Breaths	Time Taken
Muladhara	600	40 min
Swadishtana	6000	6 hours 4 mins
Manipuraka	6000	6 hours 4 mins
Anahata	6000	6 hours 4 mins
Vishuddha	1000	1 hour 6 mins 40 sec
Ajna	1000	1 hour 6 mins 40 sec
Sahasrara	1000	1 hour 6 mins 40 sec
Total	21600	24 hours

The central point for distribution of the breaths is the navel. Breath alternates between the Ida (left nostril) and Pingala (right nostril). The Ida breath is a cooling one as it is based on the moon principle while the Pingala is the heating one and represent the sun principle. The Ida and Pingala come together at the Muladhara chakra, close to the seat of the Kundalini. The Kundalini is the spot where 72000 nadis are said to congregate.

In the Chaturdasha Trikona, we observe that there is a representation of the fourteen important naadis.

Another way in which the Sri Chakra is identified with the human body is seen in the nine interlocking triangles that constitute the diagram. The nine triangles stand for the nine fundamental elements or Mula Prakruthi which are replicated in the human body as nine substances such as skin, blood, muscles, fat and bone (aspects of Shakti) and semen, marrow, vital breath and soul (aspects of Shiva).

The important marma points (locations with heightened energy) found in the human body are also represented in the Sri Chakra as the 18 marma sthanas (points that are formed by the intersection of three lines). Marma literally means "a point that can kill" and many martial art forms use these points to teach self-defence and to fatally wound an enemy. Ayurveda believes that there are 108 marma points in the body, each one serving a specific purpose. And in the Sri Chakra Yantra, these 108 points are condensed to 18 marma sthanas.

Sri Chakra and Healing

The seventh enclosure, comprising of eight triangles, is known as the remover of all diseases (Sarva Rogahara). Meditating upon this avarana can bring about overall healing as it works directly on the 18 marma points which are the main spots for the congregation of prana. The potential for healing is increased greatly when any blocks to the free movement of prana are removed.

Vedic scholars point out that specific healing of ailments related to specific body parts can be achieved by meditating upon the different avaranas. Listed below are the avaranas and their corresponding parts for the purposes of focus and meditation.

Avarana	Specific Ailment
Bhupura	Knee pain
	Joint pain
	Arthritis
	Rheumatism
	Nerve related disorders
	Alzheimer's
	Parkinson's
	Multiple Sclerosis
	Insomnia
Shodasa Dala Padma	Infertility
	Reproductive issues
	Sexual disorders

Ashta Dala Padma	Ulcers
	Digestive problems
	Irritable bowel syndrome
	Kidneys
	Pancreas (including diabetes)
	Spleen
	Gall bladder stones
	Small and large intestines
Chaturdasha	Heart disease
	Low and high blood pressure
Bahir Dasha	Skin
	Sinus
	Lungs
	Shoulder pains
	Spondylitis
Antar dasha	Psychological disorders such as
	Schizophrenia
	Anxiety
	Bipolar disorder
	Depression
	Suicidal thoughts
Ashtakona	For all kinds of chronic and acute ailments
	To rid oneself of karmic afflictions
Trikona	Cleansing and purification of all aspects of body and mind

Bindu	For spiritual ailments such as lack of belief in universe
	Addictions
	Lack of sympathy and empathy
	Excessive greed and desire
	To overcome sense of "self"

Sri Chakra and the Pineal Gland

We have discussed in an earlier chapter that certain geometric patterns bring about a change in the brain structure. Meditating on the bindu in the Sri Chakra is said to activate the pineal gland, as it compels us to bring our attention to the spot between our eyebrows.

The pineal gland is a small endocrine gland, shaped like a tiny pine cone. It derives its name from Latin "pinea" which means "pine cone." This pea-sized organ is responsible for the production of melatonin, a hormone that affects the modulation of our sleep/wake patterns, which in turn determines the production of other hormones, controls stress levels and seasonal circadian rhythms in the body.

Melatonin is also known as an anti-aging and anti-stress agent because it is involved in the dual action of suppressing cortisol and working as a powerful antioxidant.

The pineal gland is located near the centre of the brain between the two hemispheres, at the same level with the eyes which led to it being called the "third eye." In modern times, a great deal of scientific studies have been undertaken to understand the role of the pineal gland. The pineal area is covered in cerebrospinal fluid and has more blood flow per cubic volume than any other organ, making it the gland with the highest concentration of energy in the body.

In humans, the pineal cells resemble retinal cells in position and in the presence of proteins, something not found anywhere else in the body, thereby adding merit to its definition as the third eye.

Researchers have found that the pineal gland produces DMT (dimethyltriptamine). DMT is produced when the body goes through extraordinary situations such as giving birth, during sexual ecstasy, extreme physical stress and near-death experiences. It is also said to be produced during deep meditation. DMT is said to alter our dream consciousness when released into the bloodstream, during the "rapid eye movement" phase of sleep.

DMT links the body and spirit because of its relationship to visionary experiences and non-ordinary states of transcendent consciousness. This property about DMT prompted Dr. Rick Strassman to call it the Spirit Molecule. Many scientists now suggest that the pineal gland may indeed be the "seat of consciousness" based on the outcome of studies that described the role of this tiny gland - until recently considered a vestigial organ - which is of far greater importance than commonly assumed.

The connection between pineal gland and consciousness can be traced back to Egyptian, Indian and even Tibetan traditions. In Egypt, when the Pharoahs were mummified using elaborate processes of embalming and purifying, their pineal glands were removed carefully and placed in separate jars. The contents of these jar were considered as containing the gateway to the afterlife.

In India, the pineal gland is seen as the representation of the sixth *chakra (ajna),* and the ubiquitous *bindi,* which adorns a woman's forehead, is said to protect her, by blocking negative energies from reaching the third eye. *The ajna chakra* is said to be the seat of wisdom, intuition and imagination. A blocked *ajna chakra* is characterized by a lack of intuition and imagination, thereby leading to the inability to make the right decisions and inhibiting spiritual expansion and growth.

The Tibetans believe that life of an embryo begins on the 49th day after conception. It is strange that it is on the 49th day that the pineal gland starts to develop in a human embryo. This can lead us to understand why the pineal gland is considered the seat of consciousness by some experts.

The pineal gland is not protected by the blood-brain barrier and therefore it cannot defend itself against harmful toxins that enter the bloodstream. Specific toxins, such as synthetic fluoride and synthetic calcium, are shown to have an affinity with the pineal gland. These toxins weaken its abilities to produce neurotransmitters and receive photons of light from external sources.

It is important, therefore, to ensure that the pineal gland is working at its optimal capacity, in order to enjoy the benefits of spiritual growth and awareness.

10 Ways to Activate an Under-performing Pineal Gland

1. Adequate hydration and good nutrition

   Our bodies are made up of up to 75% water. Therefore, it is very important to consume adequate amounts of water to ensure activation of the pineal gland. Additionally, a balanced diet high in tryptophan is helpful in providing the building blocks for the important biochemical produced by the pineal gland. Tryptophan is found in many foods including eggs, most kinds of seeds (including sesame, chia, sunflower, pumpkin), most nuts (maximum in almonds, pistachios, hazelnuts), dark chocolate and bananas.

2. Exposure to sunlight

   Indians have been following the tradition of sun worship since Vedic times. Exposure to early morning sun stimulates the pineal gland. Exposure to sunlight is necessary for other body functions as well, and it is recommended that we spend at least 10 to 15 minutes of the day, preferably in the early morning, in the sunlight to enjoy optimal health and well-being.

3. Sleeping in complete darkness

   It is also important to note that the time spent in darkness helps the pineal gland in suppressing serotonin and increasing melatonin, which is necessary to induce sleep. A dark environment in the bedroom is very important to ensure a good night's rest.

   We should especially avoid blue light which comes from sources such as television, computer screens and smartphones. Blue light leads to the stimulation of serotonin, forcing the body to think that it is daytime, thereby upsetting the wake and sleep cycle.

4. Tapping

   Gentle tapping on the forehead in between the eyebrows activates the pineal gland. The vibration sends a wave directly to the pineal gland, activating it in the process.

5. Pressing

   Pressing the tongue against the roof of the mouth activates the pituitary gland, and through its physical and chemical connections, activates the pineal gland and hypothalamus. This method is also used in Ayurveda and Yoga, and is akin to the *kechari mudra* practised by ancient seers.

6. Staying cheerful

   Laughing and smiling help reduce stress and induce relaxation in the body, thereby increasing the flow of positive energy. Laughter leads to the release of endorphins, the feel-good hormone. Relaxation increases blood flow, which amplifies the effects of the hormones released in the body.

7. Focus and attention

   It is a well-known fact that our energy flows to wherever our attention goes. Focusing our attention on the pineal gland will help activate it.

8. Meditation and visualization

   Meditation has numerous benefits that are often written about. But one of the lesser-known benefits of mindfulness is better activation of the pineal gland. Meditating guides bio-electric energy to the pineal gland, thereby facilitating a greater sense of clarity and improving intuition.

   Visualization cannot take place without the use of the third eye. We can choose to practice any form of visualization or guided imagery to help the pineal gland become more active.

9. Chanting

   Chanting causes the tetrahedron bone in the nose to resonate, which creates a stimulation of the pineal gland. We can begin with the chanting of "Om," or any other prayer that appeals to us.

10. Ritual worship of Sri Chakra Yantra

Any ritual that involves concentration helps remove blocks and activate the pineal gland. A practice which incorporates visualization, chanting and meditation is perhaps the best way to ensure optimal functioning of the gland. Furthermore, it has been observed that focussing on one point (as we do with the bindu in the Sri Chakra) leads to a convergence of the eyeballs and energy comes to rest at the third eye, which is the seat of the pineal gland.

The physical benefits of an active pineal gland can be felt in various aspects of living such as greater balance in our work-life ratio, improved well-being, better functioning of bio-rhythms and improved hormonal states. In terms of emotional benefits, we will find that we are calmer, better at decision-making, more at peace with ourselves and others and there's a renewed zest for life.

5

SOUNDS OF THE SRI CHAKRA

"Mananaat traayate iti mantrah" – that which uplifts us by continuous repetition is a 'mantra'.

Chanting is an ancient practice that has played an integral role in all religious and spiritual traditions across the globe from time immemorial. The repeated recitation of a divine name is common to Hinduism, Islam, Christianity, Buddhism, Judaism and even in pagan and shamanic traditions. Chanting is best described as a rhythmic repetition (either silently or aloud) of a sound, word, prayer or song. It is an established fact that sound has tremendous power.

The Sanskrit word for sound is "nada." In Hindu tradition, it is believed that the entire universe is made up of sound vibrations called nada. Nada is of two types – Ahata and Anahata.

Ahata is a sound produced through contact (clapping of hands, hitting a drum, etc.), vibration (from striking the chord of a sitar or veena) and obstruction (blowing into a flute or a trumpet). While Anahata is the sound that exists in the universe as a cosmic hiss which is eternal and cannot be produced by us.

A sound, therefore, is nothing but a pulsation or vibration – a form of energy - which exists throughout the universe and can be harnessed to help align ourselves better with the higher forces of nature.

The purpose of chanting is to bring about a silence in the ever-chattering mind. The process of repetition of a word or set of words helps bring about a temporary state of mindfulness as the brain is completely absorbed in the activity of repetition. Chanting is a very useful step in the process of learning meditation as it offers a vehicle for the mind to transport itself to a higher realm.

In fact, the Sanskrit word *mantra* can be broken up into *"man"* meaning "mind" and *"tra"* meaning "tool." The vibrations created by the sound and the focus on rhythmic pronunciation have a profound effect on the body and mind. The nervous system experiences a slow down of activities and a calmness descends which reduces stress, high blood pressure and pain and improves immunity.

The ancient Vedic texts recommend the chanting of mantras as a part of spiritual practice.

Dr. David Frawley, a renowned Ayurveda expert says that "a mantra, when carefully chosen and used silently, has the ability to help alter your subconscious impulses, habits and afflictions. Mantras, when spoken or chanted, direct the healing power of prana (life force energy) and, in traditional Vedic practices, can be used to energize and access spiritual states of consciousness."

It is not necessary to learn elaborate Sanskrit verses to practice chanting. Just chanting "Om" is equally effective when done correctly. Om is considered a mantra even though it is a single word. Modern scientific studies have established that the sound of Om, when chanted, vibrates at a frequency of 432 Hz, which is said to be the frequency found throughout the universe (the humming sound of nature).

Meditation practitioners advise the use of a "beej (seed) mantra" which can be explained as our very own, personal mantra. The beej mantra is derived from the sound of each individual's nakshatra pada. The position of the moon at the time of a person's birth determines the nakshatra pada, thus making the mantra unique to that person.

In the Vedic system of astrology, there are 27 nakshatras which roughly divides the 360 degrees of zodiac into 13.2 degrees arc per nakshatra. Nakshatra refers to the lunar mansion and the 27 sectors along its ecliptic. Further, each nakshatra is divided into 4 padas.

Nakshatra and pada of an individual are determined by the position of the moon at the time of birth.

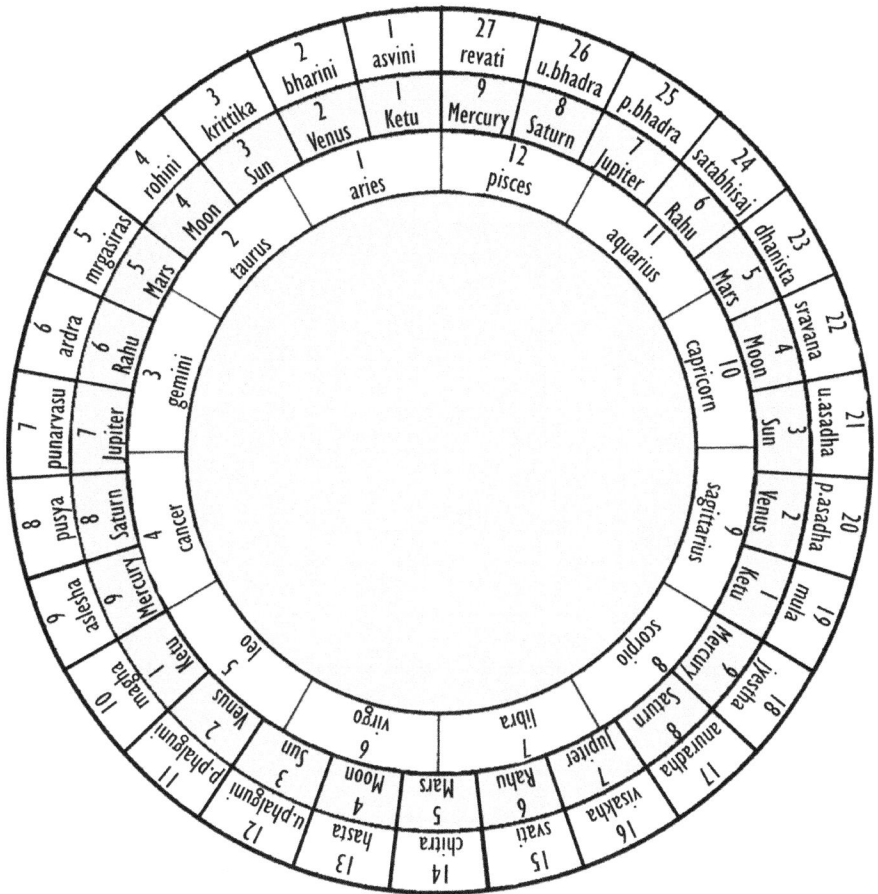

Above is a chart that contains details of the 27 nakshatras and the beej mantras associated with the 4 padas.

First, you need to find out your nakshatra and pada by looking for it on the internet. You will need your exact time, date and place of birth to arrive at the accurate nakshatra and pada.

If the nakshatra is Uttara Ashada and the pada is 1, then the bija akshara is Bhe. Adding a prefix "Om" and suffix "m" to Bhe and following it up with Namah makes a beej mantra "Om Bhem Namah".

Name of Nakshatra	Pada 1	Pada 2	Pada 3	Pada 4
Ashwini	Chu	Che	Cho	La
Bharani	Li	Lu	Le	Lo
Krittika	A	I	U	E
Rohini	O	Va	Vi	Vu
Mrigashirsha	Ve	Vo	Ka	Ke
Ardra	Ku	Gha	Na	Chha
Punarvasu	Ke	Ko	Ha	Hi
Pushya	Hu	He	Ho	Da
Ashlesha	Di	Du	De	Do
Magha	Ma	Mi	Mu	Me
Purva Phalguni	Mo	Ta	Ti	Tu
Uttara Phalguni	Te	To	Pa	Pi
Hasta	Pu	Sha	Na	Tha
Chitra	Pe	Po	Ra	Ri
Swati	Ru	Re	Ro	Ta
Vishaka	Ti	Tu	Te	To
Anuradha	Na	Ni	Nu	Ne
Jyestha	No	Ya	Yi	Yu
Moola	Ye	Yo	Bha	Bhi
Purva Ashada	Bhu	Dha	Bha	Bhi
Uttara Ashada	Bhe	Bho	Ja	Ji
Shravana	Ju	Je	Jo	Gha
Dhanishta	Ga	Gi	Gu	Ge
Shatabhisha	Go	Sa	Si	Su
Purva Bhadrapada	Se	So	Da	Di
Uttara Bhadrapada	Du	Tha	Jha	Da
Revati	De	Do	Cha	chi

Using the beej mantra helps us connect faster with the universal vibration present at the time and place of our birth. We can chant mantras at any time of the day or night - while walking, commuting, driving, cooking, trying to fall asleep or doing yoga. It is advisable to set aside a specific time for chanting away from the distractions of our daily activities.

Here are a few steps to keep in mind as you begin chanting:

* Sit up straight with your spine erect.

* Gently close the eyes and focus on your breath for a few minutes as the body begins to relax.

* At first, repeat the mantra aloud, focusing on pronunciation and duration. Make sure you chant the words at the same pace. Keep a track of the number of breaths between the words to help keep pace.

* Listen to the mantra and repeat it, allowing the words to permeate your whole being.

* Feel the vibrations as they occur within the body and be mindful of all the sensations.

* With practice, you will feel that your voice is getting deeper and gathering more power. Use this as a motivation to further the spiritual growth.

* Practice chanting every day for 10 to 15 minutes, to begin with, and then increase it to 30 minutes as the practice improves.

* You can practice with a Japa mala (similar to a rosary but with 108 beads) to help improve the meditation.

* Begin with Om and over time, make an effort to learn some of the more powerful Sanskrit mantras from a reliable source. Some of the powerful mantras are Gayatri mantra, Mahamritunjaya mantra, Shanti mantras and Dhanvantari mantra.

Chanting helps us connect with our inner self as it allows us to develop a more mindful state of awareness. Use it as a tool of higher learning for the soul and to ascend to higher spiritual dimensions.

Chanting can be especially useful at times of stress as it helps bring about a sense of calm and all-pervading positivity and offers an insight into the transience of all experiences.

Sounds of the Sri Chakra

The mantras used for meditating on the Sri Chakra are special as these mantras are demarcated from the ones that only bring about material prosperity or spiritual growth. These set of mantras are said to do both simultaneously. The Devirahasya describes how Tripurasundari is visualized as residing in the heart and how it is slowly drawn out through the breath and placed on the Yantra.

Please note that all mantras should begin with Om. The Kularnava Tantra says not beginning a mantra with Om causes impurity. The Chandrogya Tantra says that Om is closest to the Brahman; hence all worship should begin and end with it. It should also be noted that all three Vedas begin with Om.

The Sri Chakra worship is done using the following mantras and stotras:

- Bala Mantra
- Panchadasi Mantra
- Shodasi Mantra
- Sri Devi Khadgamala Stotra
- Lalitha Sahasranama
- Lalitha Trisathi

The Bala mantra is possibly one of the most potent in Sri Vidya. Practitioners are initiated into the Bala mantra before being taught the Panchadasi mantra. The presiding deity of the Bala mantra is a child goddess, shown sitting in a white flower holding a book and a japa mala (rosary).

Bala mantra can be of three types:

The basic Bala mantra that contains three bija aksharas - Aim Klim Sauh

The Bala Tripurasundari mantra that contains six bija akshara - Aim Klim Sauh Sauh Klim Aim

Bala Navaskhari mantra that contains nine bija akshara - Aim Klim Sauh Sauh Klim Aim Aim Klim Sauh

The most powerful version is considered to be the Bala Navaskari mantra because the reverse order is encased by the Bala mantra. Such an encasement is known as Samputikarana where the power, vibration and energy of the mantra are encased between two bija akshara. It is believed that reciting a mantra in the reverse order increases its power several folds. When a mantra is recited with absolute devotion and concentration, latent energy inside the body is aroused and diffused throughout the body. This diffusion is prevented by encasing the mantra between two bija aksharas.

"Aim," the first of the bija akshara is known as vaghavabija, and is said to help in perfecting knowledge. It indicates the first stage of the worship where the practitioner begins his search of Self.

The second bija "Klim" is known as kamabija, where kama means desire and the desire here is to attain the knowledge of the Goddess. The third bija "Sauh" is known as parabija, which gives power to the practitioner to realize his Self.

There are four different meditations that can be done on the Bala mantra based on the outcome sought:

- For gaining material wealth, the young form of the Goddess can be contemplated as seated in padmasana or lotus pose, holding a pomegranate and a lotus in her hands.
- For gaining knowledge, she can be visualized as one with four hands, holding a varada mudra, a pot containing nectar, a book and a abhaya mudra in each hand.
- For curing diseases, she should be meditated upon as one wearing all white garments, with her face having the lustre of the moon and her body composed of Sanskrit alphabets.
- For gaining an attractive disposition, she should be visualized with a radiant smile and dressed in regal finery, holding a noose (to captivate the attention) in her hand.

After the practice of the Bala mantra in a form that is most appealing to the seeker, the Panchadasi mantra, which is said to be the root mantra of Sri Vidya and the veritable sound-form of the Goddess, is revealed.

The Panchadasi mantra comprises of 15 bija aksharas:

Ka E Ii la Hrim

Ha Sa Ka Ha la Hrim

Sa Ka La Hrim

The mantra is divided into three kutas or peaks consisting of five syllables each. The first kuta, known as Vagbhava kuta, represents the Goddess's head; the second, known as Madhya Kuta, represents her trunk and the body from neck to navel; the third, known as Shakti kuta, represents the body below the navel.

The three kutas are shown as joined to form an inverted triangle, representing the yoni or the source of the universe.

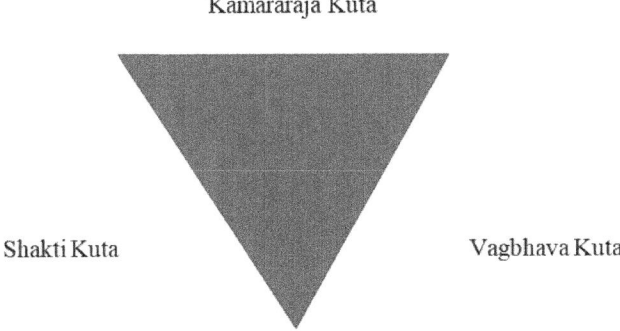

Several books are dedicated to unravel the meaning of the 15 syllables, but Vedic scholars have pointed out that it is indeed esoteric and convoluted. Hence, it is best to intuit one's own understanding of it as we progress in our sadhana. In general, the syllables are said to have the following meaning:

Ka – desire or the creation

E – Maya or the power of illusion

I – Vishnu or the divine ruling power

La – the power of bliss

Ha – space or breath

Sa – time

Ka – creation

La – bliss

Sa – time

Ka – origin

La – bliss

Hrim – repeated three times to bring about a triple transformation of our nature

This mantra is not revealed by these bījas but by the following verse in Sanskrit.

"kamo yoni: kamala vajrapanirguhahasa matarisvabhramindraa punarguhasakala mayaya ca purucyesa visvamatadividya"

This is the verse wherein the fifteen bija aksharas of the Panchadasi mantra are hidden. This is a clear indication of the highly secretive nature of this mantra. The fifteen bijas are thus:

kaman (ka) yoni: (e) kamala (i)vajrapanir (la) guha (hrim) ha (ha) sa(sa) matharisva (ka) abram (ha) indrah (la) punar guha (hrim) sakala (sa, ka, la) mayaya ca (hrim) purucyesa visvamatadividya.

The first five letters (Vagbhava Kuta) originate from the Mooladhara chakra or the root of the spine. This is where Kundalini Shakti lies dormant coiled like a snake. The first line promotes the rise of energy from the Mooladhara to the Anahata or heart chakra.

The next six letters (Kamaraja Kuta) start from the Anahata chakra and touch the Agna or the Third Eye chakra with the power and brilliance of billions of suns.

The last four letters (Shakthi Kuta) start from the Agna Chakra and touch the Sahasrara or Crown chakra with the soothing light of billions of moons.

It is said that one repetition of Panchadasi mantra is equivalent to three repetitions of Gayatri mantra.

"Om bhurbhuvaḥ svaḥ

tat saviturvareṇyaṁ

bhargo devasya dhimahi

dhiyo yo naḥ pracodayat"

The version that begins with Ka is known as the Kadi-vidya and another version that begins with Ha is known as the hadi-vidya.

Ha Sa Ka la Hrim

Ha Sa Ka Ha La Hrim

Sa Ka La Hrim

After the practice of the Panchadasi mantra, the seeker moves on to the highly secret Shodashi mantra. Shodashi refers to sixteen syllables. The bija akshara Shreem is added to the Panchadasi mantra to give us this secret, highly regarded and guarded mantra. In one Vedic text, there is a reference to giving away one's kingdom or even one's head but never to reveal the Shodashi mantra.

The reason for this secrecy is often attributed to the potency of the mantra. Lord Shiva gave 64 chakras and its mantras to mankind to help them progress in material and spiritual realms. His consort Devi was given the Sri Chakra and along with it the Shodashi mantra which contains the power of all 64 mantras put together.

The Shodasi mantra is as below:

Ka E Ii la Hrim

Ha Sa Ka Ha la Hrim

Sa Ka La Hrim

Shrim

Shrim is that which is capable of providing auspiciousness and promoting positive attitude and growth. This bija akshara is seen as inspiring faith, devotion and love in the seeker.

Once the mantras are chanted, the Sri Chakra is worshipped through a long and highly ritualistic Navavarna Puja. For those who cannot do this puja, the Vedic texts recommend the chanting of the Sri Devi Khadgamala Stotra. It condenses a long series of complicated rituals into a recitation that can be completed in a few minutes. It is advisable to recite it once a day at 8 p.m. as that is considered the most auspicious time for the Khadgamala recitation.

Stotra is a Sanskrit word that means ode, eulogy or a hymn of praise. It differs from a Shastra. A stotra is sung to a melodic tune while a shastra is recited. A stotra can be a prayer, a conversation or even a description with a poetic structure. The word comes from stu (to praise) and tra (device or instrument).

If you wish to listen to the accurate renditions of the three stotras, please check my website **www.vinitarashinkar.in** *for links to the ones which are my personal favourites.*

Khadgamala

There are myriad ways of worshipping the various deities (energies) that reside in the Sri Chakra Yantra. One of the simplest ways is by chanting the Khadgamala, which is a very powerful invocation, not just a stotra or hymn. It is considered to be a "mala mantra" (a mantra with more than

1000 letters) which invokes Sri Mahatripurasundari along with the devatas or energies that reside in various avaranas within the Sri Chakra Yantra.

The word "Khadga" means "sword" and "mala" means "garland." The Khadgamala bestows a protective garland of weapons upon those who recite it. The Khadgamala takes us on a mental journey through various avaranas of the Sri Chakra while describing the significance and meaning of the enclosures. The metaphorical journey begins at the outer periphery and culminates at the bindu. Along the way, the 98 aspects of Devi are recognized and internalized to prepare us for the final convergence of Shiva and Shakti at the bindu.

Sri Amritananda Natha explains that in the Khadgamala, the sword bestows upon its reciters the energy to transcend attachment, enabling Self-realization. He says: "the Sword [metaphorically] severs the head, separating the body from the mind. It can also be interpreted as wisdom – that which separates, categorizes and classifies. So it is a symbol of knowledge. The Khadgamala is about imagining a garland of synergistic ideas, nourishing and protecting them and putting life into them."

The correct way to chant the Khadgamala is by having an image of the yantra before us physically or visualizing it mentally if we have an accurate image stored in our mind's eye. As we recite each name, the specific portion of the yantra should be the point of focus.

The stotra begins with "*Om Aim Hrim Shrim Aim Klim Sauh*" and leads into a tribute to the Devi and the places she resides.

Hridaya Devi	Goddess who resides in the heart
Shiro Devi	Goddess who resides in the head
Shikha Devi	Goddess with flowing hair
Kavacha Devi	Goddess who is like an armour
Nethra Devi	Goddess who resides in the eyes
Astra Devi	Goddess who gives us weapons

Then the 16 aspects (nitya) or qualities of the Devi are described. These 16 qualities represent different phases of the moon, starting from the new moon (Amavasya) to the full moon (Poornima).

Kameshwari	Goddess who controls passion
Bhagamalini	Goddess who has a garland of suns
Nityaklinne	Goddess who is ever aroused
Bherunde	Goddess who is terrifying
Vahinivasini	Goddess who resides in fire
Mahavajreshwari	Goddess who is like a diamond
Shivaduti	Goddess who sends Shiva as an emissary and a bringer of joy
Twaritey	Goddess who is unstoppable
Kula Sundari	Goddess who is the most beauteous in her clan
Nitye	Goddess who is eternal
Nilapatakey	Goddess who carries a blue banner
Vijaye	Goddess who is victorious
Sarvamangale	Goddess who is completely auspicious
Jvala Malini	Goddess who is the mistress of flames
Chitre	Goddess who is like a picture
Maha Nitye	Goddess who is eternal and great

Following are the qualities that pervade Devi and the names of the saints who have worshipped her in the past:

Parameshwara Parameshwari	Goddess of the Divine God
Mitresamayi	Goddess of friendship
Sastisamayi	Goddess who is the consort of Lord Subramanya
Uddiyasamayi	Goddess who pervades as the moon does
Charyanathamayi	Goddess who pervades all rituals
Lopamudramayi	Goddess who pervades as Sage Lopamudra
Agastyamayi	Goddess who pervades as Sage Agastyamayi
Kalatapasamayi	Goddess who pervades penance over ages
Dharmacharyamayi	Goddess pervades the teachers of Dharma
Muktakeshisvarayamayi	Goddess whose hair falls freely
Dipakalanathamayi	Goddess who is like the flame of a lamp
Vishnudevamayi	Goddess who pervades God Vishnu
Prabhakaradevamayi	Goddess who pervades the Sun God
Tejodevamayi	Goddess who shines
Manojadevamayi	Goddess who pervades the God of desire
Kalyanadevamayi	Goddess who pervades God of auspiciousness
Vasudevamayi	Goddess who pervades Lord Krishna
Rathnadevamayi	Goddess who pervades the God of gems
Sriramanandamayi	Goddess who pervades the joy of Ram

Sri Chakra Yantra

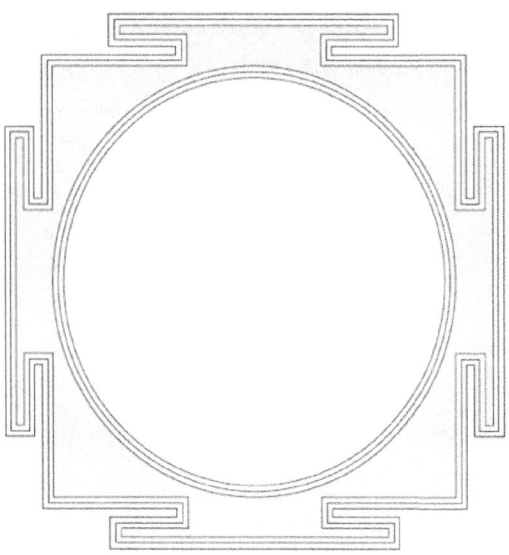

First Enclosure

Animasiddhe	Goddess who has the power to become invisible
Laghimasiddhe	Goddess who has the power to become light and fly
Garimasiddhe	Goddess who can make her body as heavy as she wants
Mahimasiddhe	Goddess who has the ability to increase or decrease the size of her body
Ishitvasiddhe	Goddess who has creative control
Vasistvasiddhe	Goddess who can command enchantingly
Prakamyasiddhe	Goddess who can realize all her desires
Bhuktisiddhe	Goddess who can enjoy all she wants
Icchasiddhe	Goddess who has powers to wish all she wants
Praptisiddhe	Goddess who can attain all that she desires
Sarvakamasiddhe	Goddess who can make us realize all desires

Brahmi	Goddess who is the power of Brahma
Maheshwari	Goddess who is the power of Shiva
Kaumari	Goddess who is the power of Subramanya
Vaishnavi	Goddess who is the power of Vishnu
Varahi	Goddess who is the power of Lord Varaha
Mahendri	Goddess who is the power of Devendra, God of Heaven
Chamunde	Goddess who killed Chanda and Munda
Mahalakshmi	Goddess Lakshmi
Sarva samkshobini	She who agitates everything
Sarva Vidravini	She who melts everything
Savrakarshini	She who attracts everything
Sarva Vasamkari	She who controls everything
Sarvonmadini	She who drives everyone mad
Sarvamahankushe	She who is the great goad to all
Sarva Khechari	She who travels through space
Sarva Beeje	She who is the seed of everything
Sarva Yoni	She who is the womb
Trilokya Mohana	She who is the mistress of all three worlds – waking, sleeping and dreaming
Chakra Swamini	Goddess of the Chakra
Prakatayogini	She who is an expert in yoga and expresses herself without inhibitions

Second Enclosure

Kamakarshini	She who attracts the power of passion
Buddhyakarshini	She who is attracted by intelligence
Ahamkarakarshini	She who attracts the power of pride
Shabdakarshini	She who is attracted by good sound
Sparshakarshini	She who is attracted by good touch
Roopakarshini	She who is attracted by good form
Rasakarshini	She who is attracted by good taste
Gandhakarshini	She who is attracted by good smell
Chittakarshini	She who is attracted by a good mind
Dhairyakarshini	She who is attracted by bravery
Smrithyakarshini	She who is attracted by good memory
Namakarshini	She who is attracted by good name
Bheejakarshini	She who is attracted by proper root mantras
Atmakarshini	She who attracts the soul
Amritakarshini	She who is attracted by immortality

Sharirakarshini	She who is attracted by the body
Sarvasha Paripuraka	Fulfiller of all desires
Chakraswamini	Goddess of the chakra
Guptayogini	Goddess who is a secret practitioner of Yoga

Third Enclosure

Anangakusume	The sentiment of flowering
Anangamekhale	The girdle of love
Anangamadane	The sentiment of arousal in love
Anangamadananture	One in the throes of love
Anangarekhe	Crossing the threshold of love
Anangavegini	The sentiment of urgency in lovemaking
Anangakushe	Goad of love
Anangamalini	Wearing a garland of love
Sarvasamkshobana	She who agitates all
Chakra Swamini	Goddess of Chakra
Guptatara Yogini	She who practices the secret yoga

Fourth Enclosure

Sarvasamkshobini	She who agitates everything
Sarvavidravini	She who makes everything liquid
Sarvakarshini	She who attracts everything
Sarva Hladini	She who makes everyone happy
Sarvasammohini	She who deludes all
Sarvastambhini	She who stops all activity
Sarva Jhrumbini	She who expands everything
Sarva Vasamkari	She who makes everyone obey
Sarvanranjini	She who makes everyone delighted
Sarvon Madini	She who makes everyone ecstatic for her
Sarvasampattipurini	She who gives all types of riches
Sarvamantramayi	She who is within all mantras
Sarvadvandvakshayankari	She who eliminates all duality
Sarvasaubhagyadayaka	She who bestows all types of luck
Chakrasvamini	Goddess of chakra
Sampradayayogini	She who practices yoga in a traditional way.

Fifth Enclosure

Sarvasiddhiprade	She who grants all occult powers
Sarvasampatprade	She who gives all kinds of riches
Sarvapriyankari	She who gives all that one wishes for
Sarvamangalakarini	She who is the harbinger of auspicious acts
Sarvakamaprade	She who fulfils all desires
Sarvadukhavimochini	She who helps rid one of all sorrows
Sarvamrityuprasamani	She who can help avoid accidental deaths
Sarvavighnanivarini	She who removes all obstacles
Sarvangasundari	She who is beautiful in her entire body
Sarvasaubhyadayani	She who gives all types of luck
Sarvarthasadaka	She who grants all objects of wealth
Chakrasvamini	Goddess of chakra
Kulottirnayayogini -	She who practices yoga to liberate the entire clan

Sixth Enclosure

Sarvajne	She who has all knowledge
Sarvashakte	She who is all powerful
Sarvaishwaryapradayini	She who gives all kinds of power to protect
Sarvajnanamayi	She who has all spiritual knowledge
Sarvavyadhivinasini	She who destroys all diseases
Sarvadharaswarupe	She who is the basis of everything
Sarvapapahare	She who destroys all sins
Sarvanandamayi	She who is full of happiness
Sarvarakshaswaroopini	She who is protector to all
Sarvekshitaphalaprade	She who gives all desired results
Sarvarakshakara-Chakrasvamini	She who protects all Goddess of chakra
Nigarbhayogini	She who like a mother protects a child in the womb

Seventh Enclosure

Vasini	She who attracts everything
Kameshwari	She who is the wife of Kameshwara (Shiva)
Modini	She who is full of joy
Vimale	She who is pure
Arune	She who is the colour of the rising sun
Jayini	She who is victorious
Sarveshwari	She who is the goddess of all
Kaulini	She who is born in a noble family
Sarvarogahara	She who destroys all diseases
Chakrasvamini	Goddess of chakra
Rahasyayogini	She who practices yoga in secret

Eighth Enclosure

Banini	She who holds an arrow
Chapini	She who holds a bow
Pasini	She who holds a rope
Ankushini	She who holds a goad
Mahakameshwari	She who is the wife of Kameshwara (Shiva)
Mahavajreshwari	She who is as strong as a diamond
Mahabhagamalini	She who wears a garland of prosperity
Sarvasiddhiprada	She who gives rise to all occult powers
Chakrasvamini	Goddess of chakra
AtiRahasyayogini	She who practices yoga in great secret

Ninth Enclosure

Sri Sri Maha Bhattarike	She who is the supreme queen
Sarvanandamaya	She who offers all kinds of happiness
Chakrasvamini	Goddess of chakra
ParaRahasyayogini	She who practices yoga in utmost secret

The nine Goddesses controlling the nine Chakras

Tripura	She who controls the three states of waking, dreaming and sleeping
Tripureshi	She who is the goddess of three worlds
Tripurasundari	She who is the most beautiful of the three worlds
Tripuravasini	She who lives in the three worlds
Tripurasiddhe	She who can make occult powers possible in three worlds
Tripuramba	She who is the mother of the three worlds
Mahatripurasundari	She who is the most beautiful
Mahamaheshwari	She who can make occult powers possible in three worlds
Mahamaharajni	She who is the great empress
Mahamahashakte	She who is the great cosmic power
Mahamahagupte	She who is the great cosmic secret
Mahamahajnapte	She who is the great cosmic memory
Mahamahaanande	She who is the great cosmic bliss
Mahamahaskandhe	She who is the great cosmic support
Mahamahashaye	She who is the great cosmic thought process
Mahamaha Srichakranagarasamrajni	The great transcendental ruler of Sri Chakra
Namaste, Namaste, Namaste Namah	I offer my Salutations.

Lalitha Sahasranama

In Hinduism, the names of deities are very useful tools in devotion. Nama strotra is based on chanting various names of a deity. Usually, the nama strotra includes 100, 108, 300 or 1000 names. The Sahasranama is a litany of a thousand names. The Lalitha Sahasranama is found in Brahmanda Purana in the form of a discussion between Hayagreeva and sage Agasthya. Hayagreeva is said to be a powerhouse of cosmic knowledge while Agasthya is a pious and powerful sage. At the request of Agasthya, Hayagreeva is believed to have taught him the thousand holiest names of Lalita.

Lalitasahasrama is a very auspicious prayer containing one thousand names of the Devi. It is said to be the only nama stotra that does not repeat a single name. Further, in order to maintain the metre, sahasranamas generally uses the artifice of adding words like tu, api, ca and hi, which are conjunctions that do not necessarily add to the meaning of the name, except in cases of interpretation. The Lalita Sahasranama does not use any such auxiliary conjunctions and is unique in being an enumeration of holy names that meets the metrical, poetical and mystic requirements of a sahasranama with its order throughout the text.

Stotras are verses praising the deity that typically begin with a dhyana shloka, which describes the deity and helps the devotee to bring the deity to mind and proceed with the meditation. Sometimes there is more than one dhyana shloka for a deity. There are 3 Dhyana shlokas in Lalita Sahasranama. I have not gone into details here as it is for the more advanced practitioner.

Meaning of the thousand names

Sahasra Nama

1	**Srimatha**	The Great Mother – this indicates her role in creation
2	**Sri maha raajnee**	She who is the empress and takes care of the universe - this indicates her role in protection
3	**Sri math simasaneshwari**	She who sits on the highest throne made of lions - this indicates her role in destruction
4	**Chidagni kunda sambootha**	She who is born from the fire of consciousness
5	**Deva karya samudhyatha**	She who is always ready to do divine work
6	**Udyath bhanu sahasrabha**	She who shines like a thousand suns
7	**Chathur baahu samanvithaa**	She who has four arms
8	**Raaga swaroopa pashaadya**	She who wields the rope of passions
9	**Krodha kara ankushojvala**	She who has anger in the form of a metal hook in one of her right hands.
10	**Mano rupeskhu kodandaa**	She whose mind is sweet like a sugar cane, which is held like a bow
11	**Pancha than mathra saayaka**	She who has five arrows of touch, smell, hearing, taste and sight
12	**Nijaruna prabha poora majjath brahmanda mandala**	She who immerses the universe in red colour like the sun at dawn

13	**Champakasoka punnaga sowgandhika lasath kacha**	She whose hair is adorned with flowers like champaka, punnaga and sowgandhika
14	**Kuru vinda mani shreni kanath kotira mandaitha**	She whose crown glitters with rows of inlaid precious stones
15	**Ashtami chandra vibhraja dhalika sthala shobhitha**	She who has a beautiful forehead like the half moon (visible on eighth day from new moon)
16	**Muka chandra kalankabha mriganabhi visheshaka**	She who has the tilak (dot) of musk on her forehead which appears like a blemish on the moon
17	**Vadana smara mangalya griha thorana chillaka**	She who has eyebrows arched like auspicious flower decorations in a festive house
18	**Vakthra lakshmi parivaha chalan meenabha lochana**	She who has beautiful eyes which look like two fishes in the pond
19	**Nava champaka pushpabha nasa dhanda virajitha**	She whose nose shines like a freshly opened flower of champaka
20	**Thara kanthi thiraskari nasabharana bhasura**	She who has a nose ring which shines like a star
21	**Kadamba manjari kluptha karna poora manohara**	She whose ears are adorned with kadamba flowers
22	**Thatanka yugali bhootha thapanodupa mandala**	She who wears the sun and the moon as ear studs

23	**Padma raaga shila darsha pari bhavi kapolabhu**	She whose cheeks shine more than a mirror made of precious gems
24	**Nava vidruma bimba sri nyakkari dashana chhada**	She whose lips are like beautiful new corals
25	**Shuddha vidyankoorakara dwija pankthi dwayojjvala**	She whose teeth shine like two lines of the brahmanas (the purest knowledge)
26	**Karpoora veeti kamodha samaakarsha diganthara**	She who gives out the fragrance of camphor or incense
27	**Nija sallapha madhurya vinirbharsitha kacchaphi**	She whose voice is sweeter than the notes of Sarawathi's veena
28	**Mandasmitha prabha poora majjat kamesha manasa**	She whose lovely smile leads the mind to dive into a river of sensuality
29	**Anaakalitha saadrushya chubuka sree virajitha**	She who has a beautiful chin comparable to nothing else
30	**Kamesha baddha mangalya sutra shobitha kandhara**	She who shines with the sacred thread tied by Shiva
31	**Kankangadha keyura kamaniya bujhanvitha**	She who is lovely with golden armlets
32	**Rathna graiveya chinthaka lola muktha phalanvitha**	She who wears a diamond necklace with moving pearls
33	**Kameswara prema rathna mani prathi pana sthani**	She who has breasts that have obtained the love of Shiva

34	**Nabhyala vala romali latha phala kucha dwayi**	She who has breasts that are like the fruit of a creeper, like the fine hair rising from her belly.
35	**Lakshya roma latha dharatha samunneya madhyama**	She whose slender waist can only be deduced from the fine hair raising from there
36	**Sthana bhara dalam madhya patta bhandha valithraya**	She who has a golden belt which appears to have been created to protect her tiny waist from her heavy breasts
37	**Arunaruna kausumba vasthra bhaswat kati thati**	She whose reddish clothes glow around her tiny waist
38	**Rathna kinkini ka ramya rasana dhama bhooshitha**	She who adorns a golden thread below her waist, decorated with bells made of precious stones
39	**Kamesha gnatha sowbhagya mardaworu dwayanvitha**	She who has tender thighs known only to Shiva
40	**Manikya mukuta kara janu dwaya virajitha**	She who has knee joints that shine like a crown studded with diamonds
41	**Indra gopa parikshiptha smarathunabha jangika**	She who has forelegs like Manmatha's case of arrows, always followed around by fireflies
42	**Kooda gulpha**	She who has well-rounded ankles
43	**Koorma prashta jayishnu prapadanvidha**	She whose feet are shaped like the back of a tortoise

Sounds of the Sri Chakra | 119

44	Nakadhi dhithi samchanna namajjana thamoguna	She who removes darkness from the mind of her devotees by the brightness of her nails
45	Pada dwaya prabha jala parakrutha saroruha	She who has two feet that are more beautiful than lotus flowers
46	Sinchana mani manjira manditha sri padaambuja	She whose anklets (filled with gem stones) make a melodious sound
47	Marali mandha gamana	She who has the gait of a swan
48	Maha lavanya shewadhi	She who is the treasure house of beauty
49	Sarvaruna	She who is golden red in all her aspects
50	Navadyangi	She who has faultless limbs
51	Sarvabharana bhooshita	She who is adorned with all ornaments
52	Shivakameswar ankastha	She who sits on the lap of Shiva
53	Shiva	She who is the personification of Shiva
54	Swadheena vallabha	She who has her husband under her control
55	Sumeru shringa madhyasta	She who lives at the centre of the peak of Mount Meru
56	Sriman- nagara nayika	She who is the chief of the city of Srinagara
57	Chinthamani grihantastha	She who lives in the wish fulfilling house
58	Pancha brahmasana sthitha	She who sits on the five aspects of brahman

59	**Maha padma tavee samstha**	She who lives in the lotus-coloured forest
60	**Kadamba vana vasini**	She who lives in the forest of kadamba
61	**Sudha sagara madhyastha**	She who lives in the midst of an ocean of nectar
62	**Kamakshi**	She who fulfils desires by her sight
63	**Kaamadaayinee**	She who grants what is desired
64	**Devarshi gana sangatha stuyamanathma vaibhava**	She who has all the qualities fit to be worshipped by sages and devas
65	**Bhandasura vadodyuktha shakthi sena samanvitha**	She who assembled an army to kill demon Bhandasura
66	**Sampathkari samarooda sindhoora vrija sevitha**	She who is surrounded by the wealth increasing elephant brigade
67	**Ashwaroodadisthi thaswa koti koti biravrutha**	She who is surrounded by millions of horse riders
68	**Chakra raja ratha rooda sarvayudha parishkritha**	She who rides the Sri Chakra chariot with all weapons
69	**Geya chakra ratha rooda manthrini pari sevitha**	She who rides in the Sri Chakra chariot with the goddess of music
70	**Kiri chakra radha rooda danda natha puraskrutha**	She who rides in the Sri Chakra chariot accompanied by the boar faced goddess

71	**Jwalamalini kakashiptha vahani prakara madhyaka**	She who resides in fort of fire built by the Goddess Jwalamalini
72	**Bhanda sainya vadodyuktha shakthi vikrama harshitha**	She who was pleased by the various Shakthis who helped in killing the army of Bhandasura
73	**Nithya parakramatopa nireekshana samutsuka**	She who is eager to see the gods who await the dawn everyday to show their valour
74	**Bhanda puthra vadodyukta balavikrama nandita**	She who was pleased by the valour of Bala Devi who destroyed the sons of Bhandasura
75	**Manthrinyamba virachitha vishanga vadha toshitha**	She who was delighted at seeing Goddess Manthrini kill Vishanga (brother of Bhandasura)
76	**Vishukra pranaharana vaaraahi veerya nandita**	She who appreciates the valour of Varahi in killing Vishuka (another brother of Bhandasura)
77	**Kameshwara mukhaloka kalpitha sri ganeshwara**	She who created Lord Ganesha by merely looking at the face of Shiva
78	**Mahaganesha nirbhinna vigna yantra praharshitha**	She who is overjoyed at seeing Lord Ganesha destroy the Vigna Yantra created by Vishuka
79	**Bhanda surendra nirmuktha sashtra prathyasthra varshini**	She who rained arrows to slay Bhandasura
80	**Karanguli nakhothpanna narayana dashakriti**	She who created the ten forms of Narayana from the tip of her nails

81	**Maha paashupathasthragni nirdagdhasura sainika**	She who destroyed the army of asuras with the great arrow of Pashupatha
82	**Kameshwarasthra nirdagdha sabandasura shunyaka**	She who destroyed Bhandasura and his city of Shunyaka with the arrow of Shiva.
83	**Brahmopendra mahendradhi deva samsthutha vaibhava**	She who is worshipped by Lord Brahma Vishnu, Indra and other devas
84	**Hara nethragni sandagdha kama sanjeevanoushadi**	She who brought back to life with Sanjeevini herb the God of love who was burnt to ashes by the fire from the third eye of Shiva
85	**Srimad vagbhava kootaika swaroopa mukha pankaja**	She whose flower like face is the residence of the goddess of Speech
86	**Kantadha kati paryantha madhya koota swaroopini**	She whose body from neck to hips represents the middle world
87	**Shakti koootaika thapanna katyatho bhaga dharini**	She whose body below the womb represents Shakti
88	**Moola manthrathmika**	She who is the soul of all mantras
89	**Moola koota thraya kalebhara**	She whose body stands for the three forms of the Supreme source
90	**Kulamruthaika rasika**	She who enjoys drinking the nectar flowing from the moon on an auspicious day

91	**Kula sanketha palini**	She who protects conventions of families
92	**Kulangana**	She who is the noblest in the family
93	**Kulanthastha**	She who is the highest in the family
94	**Kaulini**	She who is nobly born
95	**Kula yogini**	She who is the family goddess
96	**Akula**	She who is beyond family
97	**Samayantastha**	She who is the ultimate aspect of time
98	**Samayachara tatpara**	She who is devoted to time honoured traditions
99	**Muladharaika nilaya**	She who resides in the Muladhara Chakra
100	**Brahma granthi vibhedini**	She who breaks the knot of Brahma
101	**Manipurantharudita**	She who emerges in the Manipuraka Chakra
102	**Vishnu grandhi vibedhini**	She who breaks the knots of Vishnu
103	**Ajna chakranthar alastha**	She who lives at the centre of the Ajna Chakra
104	**Rudra grandhi vibhedini**	She who breaks knot of Shiva
105	**Sahasrarambhujarooda**	She who ascends/floats on the thousand petaled lotus
106	**Sudha sarabhi varshini**	She who pours out streams of nectar

107	**Tathillatha samaruchi**	She who is like a flash of lightning
108	**Shad chakropari samstitha**	She who resides above the six chakras
109	**Maha shakti**	She who is attached to the union of Shiva and Shakti
110	**Kundalini**	She who is in the form of a coiled serpent
111	**Bisa tanthu taniyasi**	She who is delicate as a lotus fibre
112	**Bhavani**	She who is the wife of Shiva
113	**Bhavanagamya**	She who can be attained through imagination
114	**Bhavaranya kutarika**	She who is like the axe used to clear the jungle of samsara
115	**Bhadrapriya**	She who is the giver of auspicious things
116	**Bhadramurthy**	She who is the embodiment of all things auspicious
117	**Bhaktha saubhagya dayini**	She who confers prosperity on her devotees
118	**Bhakthi priya**	She who is pleased by devotion
119	**Bhakthi gamya**	She who can be attained by devotion
120	**Bhakthi vasya**	She who can be won over by devotion
121	**Bhayapaha**	She who dispels fear
122	**Shambhavi**	She who is married to Shiva
123	**Sharadharadya**	She who is worshipped by Sharada (the goddess of speech)

124	**Sharvani**	She who is the consort of Shiva
125	**Sharmadayini**	She who confers happiness
126	**Shankari**	She who is the consort of Shiva
127	**Shreekari**	She who is the source of all abundance
128	**Sadhvi**	She who is pure and chaste
129	**Sharat chandra nibhanana**	She who has a face like moon in the autumn
130	**Shatho dari**	She who has a soft waist
131	**Shanthimati**	She who personified peace
132	**Niradhara**	She who does not depend on anyone
133	**Niranjana**	She who is devoid of all blemishes
134	**Nirlepa**	She who does not have any attachment
135	**Nirmala**	She who is the personification of clarity
136	**Nitya**	She who is eternal
137	**Nirakara**	She who has no form
138	**Nirakula**	She who is free from confusion
139	**Nirguna**	She who is without sattva, rajas and tamas
140	**Nishkala**	She who is indivisible
141	**Shanta**	She who is peaceful and serene
142	**Nishkama**	She who does not have any desires
143	**Niruppallava**	She who is imperishable

144	**Nitya mukta**	She who is forever free from the ties of the world
145	**Nirvikara**	She who is free from imperfections
146	**Nishprapancha**	She who is beyond this world
147	**Nirashraya**	She who does not need shelter
148	**Nitya shuddha**	She who is eternally auspicious
149	**Nitya buddha**	She who is forever wise
150	**Niravadhya**	She who is beyond reproach
151	**Nirantara**	She who is without barriers
152	**Nishkaarana**	She who is without cause
153	**Nishkalanka**	She who does not have flaws
154	**Nirupadhi**	She who does not have any basis
155	**Nireeshwara**	She who has no superior
156	**Neeraga**	She who has no desires
157	**Raga madani**	She who suppresses desires
158	**Nirmada**	She who is free from conceit
159	**Madanasini**	She who destroys pride and conceit
160	**Nischintha**	She who is never worried
161	**Nirahankara**	She who does not have an ego
162	**Nirmoha**	She who is free from delusion
163	**Mohanashini**	She who is the destroyer of delusion
164	**Nirmama**	She who has no selfishness
165	**Mamata hanthri**	She who destroys selfishness
166	**Nishpapa**	She who is sinless

167	**Papa nashini**	She who destroys sin
168	**Nishkrodha**	She who is devoid of anger
169	**Krodha shamani**	She who destroys anger
170	**Nir lobha**	She who is not greedy
171	**Lobha nasini**	She who removes greed
172	**Nissamshaya**	She who is free from doubt
173	**Samshayagni**	She who dispels doubts
174	**Nirbhava**	She who does not have birth
175	**Bhava nashini**	She who is the destroyer of sorrow of samsara
176	**Nirvikalpa**	She who is unwavering and without conflicts
177	**Nirabadha**	She who is not disturbed by anything
178	**Nirbhedha**	She who is without duality
179	**Bhedha nashini**	She who destroys all duality
180	**Nirnasha**	She who is indestructible
181	**Mrityu mathani**	She who is the controller of death
182	**Nishkriya**	She who is free from work
183	**Nishparigraha**	She who does not accept anything from others
184	**Nisthula**	She who is incomparable
185	**Nila chikura**	She who has shining black hair
186	**Nirpaya**	She who is never destroyed
187	**Nirathyaya**	She who cannot be transgressed
188	**Durlabha**	She who is not easy to obtain

189	**Durgama**	She who is difficult to approach
190	**Durga**	She who is the virgin Goddess Durga
191	**Dukha hanthri**	She who destroys sorrows
192	**Sukha prada**	She who gives pleasures and happiness
193	**Dushta doora**	She who keeps away from evil
194	**Durachara shamani**	She who destroys evil practices
195	**Dosha varjitha**	She who is devoid of impurities
196	**Sarvagya**	She who knows everything
197	**Saandra karuna**	She who is full of compassion
198	**Samanadhika varjitha**	She who is without any equal
199	**Sarvashakthimayi**	She who is the universal energy
200	**Sarvamangala**	She who is universal auspiciousness
201	**Sadgathiprada**	She who shows the path of truth
202	**Sarveshwari**	She who is goddess of all
203	**Sarvamayi**	She who is everywhere
204	**Sarva manthra swaroopini**	She who is the personification of all mantras
205	**Sarva yanthrathmika**	She who is the hidden power of all yantras
206	**Sarva tanthra roopa**	She who is also goddess of all tantras
207	**Manonmani**	She who is a deluder of the mind
208	**Maaheswari**	She who is the consort of Shiva
209	**Mahadevi**	She who is the consort of Shiva

210	**Mahalakshmi**	She who is the great Goddess Lakshmi
211	**Mridapriya**	She who is beloved to Shiva
212	**Maharoopa**	She who has a huge form
213	**Mahapoojya**	She who is worthy of being worshipped
214	**Maha pathaka nashini**	She who destroys mortal sins
215	**Mahamaya**	She who is the great illusion
216	**Mahasattva**	She who is filled with purity
217	**Mahashakthi**	She who has great power
218	**Maharathi**	She who gives great conjugal bliss
219	**Maha bhoga**	She who enjoys great pleasures
220	**Mahaiswarya**	She who has great wealth
221	**Mahaveerya**	She who has great virility
222	**Mahabala**	She who is very strong
223	**Mahabuddhi**	She who is of superior intellect
224	**Mahasiddhi**	She who is supreme attainment
225	**Maha yogeshwareshwari**	She who is goddess of yoga
226	**Mahatantra**	She who is the goddess of tantra
227	**Mahamantra**	She who is the supreme chant
228	**Mahayantra**	She who is the most auspicious Sri Chakra Yantra
229	**Mahaasana**	She who sits on the highest throne
230	**Maha yaga kramaradhya**	She who is worthy of worship with yagnas

231	**Maha bhairava poojitha**	She who is worshipped by Shiva
232	**Maheshwara mahakalpa maha tandava sakshini**	She who is witness to the dance of Shiva at the end of creation
233	**Maha kamesha mahishi**	She who is the prime consort of Shiva
234	**Maha tripura sundari**	She who is the beauty of the three cities and three worlds
235	**Chathu shasti upacharadhya**	She who should be worshipped with sixty-four rituals
236	**Chathu shasti kala mayi**	She who is well-versed with the sixty-four arts
237	**Maha chathu shasti koti yogini gana sevitha**	She who is being worshipped by the sixty-four crore yoginis
238	**Manu vidya**	She who is the knowledge of Manu dharma shastra
239	**Chandra vidya**	She who is the embodiment of lunar knowledge
240	**Chandra mandala madhyaga**	She who is in the center of the moon's sphere
241	**Charuroopa**	She who is most beautiful
242	**Charuhasa**	She who has a beautiful smile
243	**Charuchandra kaladhara**	She who wears the beautiful crescent moon
244	**Charachara jagannatha**	She who is the lord of which moves and that which is immobile
245	**Chakraraja niketana**	She who lives in the Sri Chakra

246	**Parvathi**	She who is the daughter of the mountain
247	**Padmanayana**	She who is lotus-eyed
248	**Padmaraga samaprabha**	She who shines like a padmaraga gem
249	**Panchapretasanaseena**	She who sits on the seat formed by five corpses
250	**Panchabrahma swaroopini**	She who gives form to the five aspects of brahman
251	**Chinmayi**	She who is pure consciousness
252	**Paramananda**	She who is supremely happy
253	**Vignana ganaroopini**	She who is the personification of liberating knowledge
254	**Dhyana dhyathru dhyeya roopa**	She who represents the subject and object of meditation
255	**Dharmadharma vivarjitha**	She who has transcended justice and injustice
256	**Vishwa roopa**	She who has an universal form
257	**Jagarini**	She who is always awake
258	**Svapanthi**	She who is in a state of dreaming
259	**Taijasathmika**	She who is the soul of a jiva in the state of deep sleep
260	**Suptha**	She who is in a state of deep sleep
261	**Prajnatmika**	She who is not separate from deep sleep
262	**Turya**	She who is in the state of ultimate realization

263	**Sarvavastha vivarjitha**	She who transcends all states
264	**Srishtikarthri**	She who is the creator
265	**Brahmaroopa**	She who is the form of brahma
266	**Gopthri**	She who protects
267	**Govindaroopini**	She who has assumed the form of Govinda
268	**Samharini**	She who is the destroyer of the universe
269	**Rudra roopa**	She who assumes the form of Shiva
270	**Thirodhana kari**	She who conceals the reality
271	**Eeshwari**	She who is a consort of Shiva
272	**Sadashiva**	She who is of the form of Sadashiva
273	**Anugrahada**	She who gives blesses
274	**Panchakrithya parayana**	She who is responsible for the five universal tasks of creation, preservation, concealment, revelation and destruction
275	**Bhanu mandala madhyastha**	She who is at the centre of the sun
276	**Bhairavi**	She who is the consort of Shiva
277	**Bhagamalini**	She who controls the female reproductive system
278	**Padmasana**	She who sits in the lotus pose
279	**Bhagavathi**	She who is the giver of all abundance
280	**Padmanabha sahodari**	She who is the sister of Vishnu

281	**Unmesha nimishotpanna vipanna bhuvanavali**	She who creates and destroys worlds in the time taken to open and close her eyelids
282	**Sahasra seersha vadana**	She who has thousands of heads and faces
283	**Sahasrakshi**	She who has thousands of eyes
284	**Sahasrapath**	She who has thousands of feet
285	**Aabrahma keeta janani**	She who has created all forms of life from insects to Brahman
286	**Varnashrama vidhayini**	She who created the four-fold division of society
287	**Nijajna roopa nigama**	She who gives orders based on Vedas
288	**Punyapunya phala prada**	She who grants fruit of good and bad actions
289	**Shruti seemantha sindhoorikritha padabjha dhoolika**	The dust from whose feet is the sindoor filling up the hair parting of the mother of Vedas
290	**Sakalagama sandoha shukthi samputa maukthika**	She who is the pearl seated in the shell of the scriptures
291	**Purushartha pradha**	She who fulfils the four objects of human life – dharma, artha, kama and moksha
292	**Poorna**	She who is complete
293	**Bhogini**	She who enjoys pleasures
294	**Bhuvaneshwari**	She who is the goddess of the universe
295	**Ambika**	She who is the mother of the world

296	**Anadi nidhana**	She who has neither beginning nor end
297	**Hari brahmendra sevitha**	She who is worshipped by Vishnu, Indra and Brahma
298	**Naarayani**	She who is female counterpart of Narayana
299	**Naada roopa**	She who is the form of sound
300	**Nama roopa vivarjitha**	She who has shed all name and form
301	**Hrimkari**	She who is the holy syllable hrim
302	**Hreemathi**	She who is endowed with modesty
303	**Hrudya**	She who is the heart
304	**Heyopadeya varjitha**	She who does not have aspects which can be accepted or rejected
305	**Raja rajarchitha**	She who is worshipped by king of kings
306	**Ragni**	She who is the queen of Shiva
307	**Ramya**	She who is pleasant
308	**Rajeeva lochana**	She who is lotus-eyed
309	**Ranjani**	She who delights all
310	**Ramani**	She who gives joy
311	**Rasya**	She who is the sap of all
312	**Ranath kinkini mekhala**	She who wears the golden waistband with tinkling bells
313	**Ramaa**	She who brings good fortune

314	**Raakendu vadana**	She who has a face like the full moon
315	**Rathi roopa**	She who is like the wife of Kama
316	**Rathi priya**	She who is the enjoyer of conjugal bliss
317	**Rakshaa kari**	She who protects
318	**Rakshasagni**	She who kills demons
319	**Raamaa**	She who is feminine
320	**Ramana lampata**	She who enjoys romancing her husband
321	**Kaamya**	She who is desirable
322	**Kamakala roopa**	She who represents the art of sex
323	**Kadambha kusuma priya**	She who is fond of kadamba flowers
324	**Kalyani**	She who is auspicious
325	**Jagathikandha**	She who is the root of the world
326	**Karuna rasa sagara**	She who is an ocean of mercy
327	**Kalavathi**	She who excels in all arts
328	**Kalaalapa**	She who has a pleasing voice
329	**Kaantha**	She who glitters
330	**Kadambari priya**	She who likes the intoxicant kadambari
331	**Varada**	She who gives boons
332	**Vama nayana**	She who has beautiful eyes
333	**Vaaruni madavihvala**	She who gets intoxicated with the drink of happiness
334	**Viswadhika**	She who is above the universe

335	**Veda vedya**	She who stands for the knowledge of Vedas
336	**Vindhyachala nivasini**	She who lives in the Vindhyachala mountains
337	**Vidhatri**	She who carries the world
338	**Veda janani**	She who is the mother of the Vedas
339	**Vishnu maya**	She who is the deluding power of Vishnu
340	**Vilasini**	She who loves pleasure and enjoyment
341	**Kshetra swaroopa**	She who is the personification of the body
342	**Kshetreshi**	She who is the goddess of the body
343	**Kshetra kshetrajna palini**	She who is the ruler of the body and self
344	**Kshaya vridhi vinirmuktha**	She who is free from growth and decay
345	**Kshetra pala samarchitha**	She who is worshipped by Shiva in an infant's form
346	**Vijaya**	She who is victorious
347	**Vimala**	She who is free from ignorance
348	**Vandya**	She who is venerable
349	**Vandharu jana vatsala**	She who has affection towards all those who worship her
350	**Vaag vadhini**	She who excels in debates
351	**Vama keshi**	She who has beautiful hair

352	**Vahni mandala vaasini**	She who resides in the sphere of fire
353	**Bhakthi mat kalpa lathika**	She who is the wish-granting creeper
354	**Pashu pasha vimochani**	She who releases living beings from bondage
355	**Samhrutha sesha pashanda**	She who destroys people who have no faith
356	**Sadachara pravarthika**	She who makes things happen through good conduct
357	**Thapathrayagni santhapta samahladana chandrika**	She who is like moonshine and suffers the three fires
358	**Tharuni**	She who is eternally young
359	**Thapasa aradhya**	She who is worshipped by sages
360	**Thanu madhya**	She who has a slender waist
361	**Thamopaha**	She who removes tamas guna
362	**Chithi**	She who is pure consciousness
363	**Thatpada lakshyartha**	She who is the embodiment of truth
364	**Chideka rasa roopini**	She who is the nature of pure intellect
365	**Swathmananda lavibhootha brahmadya ananda santhathi**	She who makes the bliss of Brahma look insignificant in comparison to her own
366	**Paraa**	She who transcends all
367	**Prathyak chithi roopa**	She who is the nature of the unmanifested consciousness

368	**Pashyanti**	She who is the second level of sound after paraa
369	**Paradevatha**	She who gives power to gods
370	**Madhyama**	She who is in the middle of everything
371	**Vaikhari roopa**	She who is sound in an audible form
372	**Bhakta manasa hamsika**	She who is like a swan in the lake of the mind
373	**Kameshwara prana nadi**	She who is the essence of Shiva
374	**Kruthagna**	She who commands all actions
375	**Kama poojitha**	She who is worshipped by the god of love
376	**Shringara rasa sampoorna**	She who is full of the passion of love
377	**Jayaa**	She who is the personification of victory
378	**Jalandhara sthitha**	She who is on the seat of learning
379	**Odyana peetha nilaya**	She who resides in a prescribed order
380	**Bindu mandala vaasini**	She who lives in the dot at the centre of the Sri Chakra
381	**Raho yaga kramaradhya**	She who can be worshipped by secret tantra rituals
382	**Rahastarpana tarpitha**	She who is gratified by the secret rites of worship
383	**Sadya prasadini**	She who bestows her grace instantly

384	**Viswa sakshini**	She who is the witness to the universe
385	**Sakshi varjitha**	She who does not have a witness for herself
386	**Shadanga devatha yuktha**	She who has six deities as body parts
387	**Shadgunya paripooritha**	She who is endowed with six qualities of wealth, bravery, fame, wisdom, prosperity and dispassion
388	**Nitya klinna**	She who is always compassionate
389	**Nirupama**	She who is without comparison
390	**Nirvana sukhadayini**	She who gives the bliss of liberation
391	**Nithya shodashika roopa**	She who is of the form of sixteen goddesses
392	**Srikandardha sareerini**	She who occupies half the body of Shiva
393	**Prabhavathi**	She who is effulgent
394	**Prabha roopa**	She who personifies light
395	**Prasiddha**	She who is famous
396	**Parameshwari**	She who is the ultimate goddess
397	**Mulaprakrithi**	She who is of primordial nature
398	**Avyaktha**	She who is unmanifested
399	**Vykta avyakta swaroopini**	She who is visible and invisible
400	**Vyapini**	She who is all-pervading
401	**Vividhakara**	She who has several forms

402	**Vidya avidya swaroopini**	She who is both knowledge as well as ignorance
403	**Maha kamesha nayana kumuda ahladha kaumudi**	She who is the moonlight that opens the lotus-like eyes of Shiva
404	**Bhaktha hardha thamo bedha bhanu mat bhanu santhathi**	She who is like sunrays that remove the darkness from the minds of devotees
405	**Shivaduthi**	She who is a messenger of Shiva
406	**Shivaradhya**	She who is worshipped by Lord Shiva
407	**Shivamoorthi**	She who is of the form of Lord Shiva
408	**Shivankari**	She who is the cause of the auspiciousness
409	**Shivapriya**	She who is dear to Shiva
410	**Shivapara**	She who is dedicated to none other than Shiva
411	**Shishteshta**	She who is of virtuous conduct
412	**Shishta poojitha**	She who is being worshipped by the virtuous
413	**Aprameya**	She who cannot be measured
414	**Swaprakasha**	She who has her own luster
415	**Mano vachama gochara**	She who is beyond the mind and speech
416	**Chichchakti**	She who is the power of consciousness
417	**Chethanaroopa**	She who is dynamic
418	**Jada shakthi**	She who is static energy

419	**Jadathmika**	She who is the hidden power of inert matter
420	**Gayathri**	She who is the Gayathri mantra
421	**Vyahruthi**	She who is the nature of utterance
422	**Sandhya**	She who is the twilight
423	**Dwija brinda nishewitha**	She who is being worshipped by the twice born
424	**Tattvasana**	She who is seated on the principles of creation
425	**Tat**	She who is that or the supreme truth
426	**Twam**	She who is us
427	**Ayee**	She who is the mother
428	**Pancha koshanthara sthitha**	She who is in the five bodily sheaths
429	**Nisseema mahima**	She who is limitless
430	**Nithya yauvana**	She who is eternally young
431	**Mada shalini**	She who shines by her exuberance
432	**Madha ghurnitha rakthakshi**	She who has red eyes, rolling with rapture
433	**Madha patala gandabu**	She who has cheeks that are red with rapture
434	**Chandana drava dhigdhangi**	She whose body is smeared with sandal paste
435	**Champeya kusuma priya**	She who likes the flowers of champaka tree
436	**Kushala**	She who is skillful

437	**Komalaakara**	She who has soft beautiful form
438	**Kuru kulla**	She who is of the form of Goddess Kurukulla
439	**Kuleshwari**	She who is the goddess for the clan
440	**Kula kundalaya**	She who is the power of the Kundalini
441	**Kaula marga thath para sevitha**	She who is being worshipped by those devoted to kaula tradition
442	**Kumara gana nathambha**	She who is the mother to Ganesha and Subramanya
443	**Thushti**	She who is the personification of happiness
444	**Pushti**	She who is the personification of health
445	**Mathi**	She who is the personification of wisdom
446	**Dhrithi**	She who is the personification of fortitude
447	**Shanti**	She who is peaceful
448	**Svasthimati**	She who always keeps herself fit
449	**Kanthi**	She who is the personification of light
450	**Nandini**	She who gives delight
451	**Vigna nashini**	She who removes obstacles
452	**Tejovathi**	She who shines
453	**Trinayana**	She who has three eyes of sun, moon and fire

454	**Lolakshi kama roopini**	She who is the passion in the roving eyes
455	**Malini**	She who wears a garland
456	**Hamsini**	She who is surrounded by swans
457	**Mata**	She who is the mother
458	**Malayachala vasini**	She who lives in the Malaya mountain
459	**Sumukhi**	She who has a pleasant face
460	**Nalini**	She who is tender
461	**Subru**	She who has beautiful eyebrows
462	**Shobhana**	She who brings lustre to things
463	**Sura nayika**	She who is the leader of gods
464	**Kalakanti**	She who is the consort of Shiva
465	**Kanthimati**	She who has lustre
466	**Kshobhini**	She who creates upheaval in the mind
467	**Sukshma roopini**	She who is subtle
468	**Vajreshwari**	She who is the goddess of diamonds
469	**Vamadevi**	She who is the consort of Shiva
470	**Vayovastha vivarjitha**	She who does not change with age
471	**Siddeshwari**	She who is the goddess of supernatural powers
472	**Siddha vidya**	She who has knowledge of siddhas
473	**Siddha matha**	She who is the mother of siddhas

474	**Yashaswini**	She who is unequalled and renown
475	**Vishudhi chakra nilaya**	She who resides in the Visuddha Chakra
476	**Rakthavarna**	She who is of a rosy complexion
477	**Trilochana**	She who has three eyes
478	**Khadvangadhi praharana**	She who strikes with a sword
479	**Vadanaika samanvitha**	She who has only one face (no deceptions)
480	**Payasanna priya**	She who likes sweet rice
481	**Thvak-stha**	She who is the presiding deity of skin or the sense of touch
482	**Pashu loka bhayankari**	She who invokes fear in the mind of the ignorant
483	**Amruthadi maha shakti samvritha**	She who is surrounded by the maha shakthis
484	**Dakineeshwari**	She who is goddess of death
485	**Anahathabja nilaya**	She who lives in the anahata chakra
486	**Shyamabha**	She who is black in colour
487	**Vadanadwaya**	She who has two faces (pleasant and unpleasant)
488	**Damshtrojwala**	She who has fang like teeth
489	**Aksha maladhi dhara**	She who wears a rosary of rudraksh beads
490	**Rudhira samsthida**	She who abides in the blood stream of beings

491	**Kalarathryadhi shakt yogavritha**	She who is surrounded by shakthis like Kalarathri and others
492	**Snigdhaudana priya**	She who likes oily foods
493	**Maha veerendra varadha**	She who grants boons to great kings who worship her
494	**Rakinyambha swaroopini**	She who is the form of Rakini
495	**Manipoorabja nilaya**	She who abides in the Manipura Chakra
496	**Vadanathraya samyutha**	She who has three faces (Saraswati, Lakshmi and Parvathi)
497	**Vajradhikayudhopetha**	She who has weapons like Vajrayudha
498	**Damaryadhibhi ravrutha**	She who is surrounded by goddesses like Damari
499	**Rakta varna**	She who is of the colour of blood
500	**Mamsa nishta**	She who is found in the flesh as energy
501	**Gudanna preetha manasa**	She who likes a sweet rice preparation
502	**Samastha bhaktha sukhadha**	She who gives pleasure to all her devotees
503	**Lakinyambha swaroopini**	She who is famous in the form of "Lakini"
504	**Swadhishtanambujagatha**	She who lives in the Swasthithana Chakra

505	**Chathur vakthra manohara**	She who has four beautiful faces
506	**Shuladyudha sampanna**	She who has a spear as her weapon
507	**Peetha varna**	She who is of golden colour
508	**Athigarvitha**	She who is very proud
509	**Medhonishta**	She who can be found in the fatty layers of the body as energy
510	**Madhu preetha**	She who likes honey
511	**Bandinyadhi samanvitha**	She who is accompanied by the Bandini shaktis
512	**Dadhyanna saktha hridhaya**	She who likes curd rice
513	**Kakini roopa dharini**	She who takes the form of "Kakini"
514	**Muladarambujarudha**	She who resides in the Mooladhara Chakra
515	**Pancha vakthra**	She who has five faces
516	**Sthithi samsthitha**	She who is in the bones as marrow
517	**Ankushadi praharana**	She who holds a weapon called the Ankusha
518	**Varadaadi nishevitha**	She who is surrounded by Varada and other goddesses
519	**Mudgau danasaktha chitta**	She who likes food that contains green gram dhal
520	**Sakinyambha swaroopini**	She who is in the form of "Sakini"

521	**Ajna chakrabja nilaya**	She who resides in the Ajna Chakra
522	**Shukla varna**	She who is white coloured
523	**Shadanana**	She who has six faces
524	**Majja samstha**	She who located in the bone marrow
525	**Hamsavathi mukhya shakthi samanvitha**	She who is surrounded by shakthis such as Hamsavathi
526	**Haridrannaika rasika**	She who likes rice mixed with turmeric
527	**Hakini roopa dharini**	She who has the form of "Hakini"
528	**Sahasra dala padmastha**	She who resides in the Sahsrara Chakra
529	**Sarva varnopi shobitha**	She who shines in all colours
530	**Sarva-ayudha dhara**	She who is armed with all weapons
531	**Shukla samsthitha**	She who is located in the semen
532	**Sarvathomukhi**	She who has faces everywhere
533	**Sarvoudhana preetha chittha**	She who likes all types of rice
534	**Yakinyambha swaroopini**	She who takes the form of "yakini"
535	**Swaha**	She who is the personification of the offering mantra "swaha"
536	**Svadha**	She who is the offering made to each god
537	**Amathi**	She who is mindless

538	**Medha**	She who is brilliant
539	**Shruthi**	She who is the Vedas
540	**Smrithi**	She who is the guide to the Vedas
541	**Anuthama**	She who is excellent
542	**Punya keerthi**	She who is famous for good deeds
543	**Punya labhya**	She who can be attained by good deeds
544	**Punya shravana keerthana**	She who gives abundantly to those who listen and sing about her
545	**Pulomajarchidha**	She who is worshipped by the wife of Indra
546	**Bandhamochini**	She who releases from bondage
547	**Barbaralaka**	She who has forelocks which resembles waves
548	**Vimarsha roopini**	She who is the reflection
549	**Vidya**	She who is learning
550	**Viyadhadi jagatprasu**	She who created the earth and the sky
551	**Sarva vyadhi prashamani**	She who cures all diseases
552	**Sarva mrutyu nivarini**	She who prevents all types of deaths
553	**Agraganya**	She who is the foremost of all
554	**Achintyaroopa**	She who is beyond thought
555	**Kali kalmasha nashini**	She who destroys evils of the dark age

556	Kathyayini	She who is Kathyayini
557	Kala hanthri	She who dissolves time
558	Kamalaksha nishevitha	She who is worshipped by the lotus-eyed Vishnu
559	Thamboola pooritha mukhi	She whose mouth is filled with betel leaves and betel nut
560	Daadimi kusuma prabha	She whose colour is like that of the pomegranate bud
561	Mrigakshi	She who has eyes like deer
562	Mohini	She who bewitches
563	Mukhya	She who is the One
564	Mridani	She who gives pleasure
565	Mithra roopini	She who is of the form of sun
566	Nithya Truptha	She who is always content
567	Bhakta Nidhi	She who is the treasure of her devotees
568	Niyanthri	She who controls
569	Nikhileswari	She who is goddess of everything
570	Maitryadhi vasana labhya	She who can be attained by habits such as friendship
571	Maha-pralaya sakshini	She who is a witness to the great deluge
572	Parashakthi	She who is the absolute energy
573	Paranishta	She who is absorbed in the transcendant
574	Pragyana-gana roopini	She who is the personification of all superior knowledge

575	**Madhvi-pana lasaa**	She who enjoys the intoxicating drink Madhvi
576	**Matha**	She who is inebriated
577	**Mathruka varna roopini**	She who represents the syllable "Aa"
578	**Maha kailasa nilaya**	She who resides in Kailasa
579	**Mrinala mrudhu dhorllatha**	She who has arms as tender as a lotus stalk
580	**Mahaneeya**	She who is fit to be venerated
581	**Daya moorthi**	She who is the personification of mercy
582	**Maha samrajya shalini**	She who is the chief of all the worlds
583	**Atmavidya**	She who is the knowledge of the soul
584	**Maha vidya**	She who is the great knowledge
585	**Srividya**	She who is the knowledge of the Mother Goddess
586	**Kama sevitha**	She who is worshipped by/as the God of love
587	**Sri shodasakshari vidya**	She who is the knowledge of sixteen-lettered mantra
588	**Trikuta**	She who is the mountain with three peaks
589	**Kama kotika**	She who sits on Kama Koti peetha
590	**Kataksha kimkari bhootha kamala koti sevitha**	She who is attended to by a multitude of Lakshmis who yearn for her glance
591	**Shira sthitha**	She who is located in the head

592	**Chandra nibha**	She who is like the full moon
593	**Phalasthendra**	She who is in the forehead of Indra
594	**Dhanu prabha**	She who is like the rainbow
595	**Hridayastha**	She who is in the heart
596	**Ravi pragya**	She who has the lustre of the sun
597	**Trikonanthara deepika**	She who is like light in a triangle
598	**Dakshayani**	She who is the daughter of Daksha
599	**Daithya hanthri**	She who kills the demons
600	**Daksha yagna vinashini**	She who destroys the sacrifice conducted by Daksha
601	**Darandolitha deergakshi**	She who has long eyes that move a little
602	**Darahasojwalanmukhi**	She who has a face that shines with her smile
603	**Guru moorthi**	She who is the form of a teacher
604	**Gunanidhi**	She who is the treasure house of good qualities
605	**Gomatha**	She who is the mother cow
606	**Guhajanmabhu**	She who is the mother of Subrahmanya
607	**Deveshi**	She who is the ruler of gods
608	**Danda neethistha**	She who judges and punishes
609	**Daharakasha roopini**	She who is of the form of wide sky

610	**Prathi panmukhya rakantha thithi mandala poojitha**	She who is worshipped on all the fifteen days, from new moon to full moon
611	**Kalathmika**	She who is the soul of all arts
612	**Kala natha**	She who is a supporter of all arts
613	**Kavya labha vimodhini**	She who enjoys poetry
614	**Sachamara rama vani savya dakshina sevitha**	She who is being fanned by Lakshmi, the goddess of wealth and Saraswathi, the goddess of knowledge
615	**Adishakthi**	She who is the primeval force
616	**Ameya**	She who cannot be measured
617	**Atma**	She who is the soul
618	**Parama**	She who is supreme
619	**Pavana krithi**	She who is of sacred form
620	**Aneka koti brahmanda janani**	She who is the mother of several billions of universes
621	**Divya vigraha**	She who has a divine form
622	**Klim karee**	She who is the shape of "Klim"
623	**Kevala**	She who is she herself
624	**Guhya**	She who is to be known in secret
625	**Kaivalya pada dhayini**	She who grants redemption
626	**Tripura**	She who lives in the three aspects
627	**Trijagat vandhya**	She who is worshipped by the three worlds

628	**Trimurti**	She who is the three aspects of the Supreme Being
629	**Tridasheshwari**	She who is the goddess for all gods
630	**Tryakshari**	She who is of the form of three syllables (A, U, M)
631	**Divya gandhadya**	She who has a godly smell
632	**Sindhura thila kanchita**	She who wears the red dot on her forehead
633	**Uma**	She who is in Om
634	**Shailendra thanaya**	She who is the daughter of the king of mountains
635	**Gowri**	She who has a fair complexion
636	**Gandharva sevitha**	She who is attended by Gandharvas
637	**Vishwa garbha**	She who is the womb of the universe
638	**Swarna garbha**	She whose womb is golden
639	**Avarada**	She who punishes the ignorant
640	**Vagadeeshwari**	She who is the goddess of speech
641	**Dhyanagamya**	She who can be attained by meditation
642	**Aparichedya**	She whose whereabouts cannot be ascertained
643	**Jnaanada**	She who gives out knowledge
644	**Jnana vigraha**	She who is the personification of knowledge

645	**Sarva vedanta samvedya**	She who can be known by all Upanishads
646	**Satyananda swaroopini**	She who is the personification of truth and bliss
647	**Lopamudrarchitha**	She who is worshipped by Lopa Mudhra, the wife of Agasthya
648	**Leela kluptha brahmanda mandala**	She who creates different universes by simple play
649	**Adrishya**	She who cannot be seen
650	**Drishya rahitha**	She who is without the visible
651	**Vignathree**	She who knows all sciences
652	**Vedhya varjitha**	She who does not need to learn anything
653	**Yogini**	She who is the personification of yoga
654	**Yogadha**	She who gives knowledge and experience of yoga
655	**Yogya**	She who is worthy of practising yoga
656	**Yogananda**	She who is the bliss arising from yoga
657	**Yugandhara**	She who upholds the ages
658	**Icchashakthi gnanashakthi kriyashakthi swaroopini**	She who embodies the power of intention, knowledge and actions
659	**Sarvaadhara**	She who is the support to all
660	**Supratishta**	She who is well-established
661	**Sadasadroopa dharini**	She who assumes both true and false aspects

662	**Ashta moorthi**	She who has eight forms
663	**Ajajaithree**	She who has won over ignorance
664	**Loka yathra vidahyini**	She who sets the world in motion
665	**Ekakini**	She who is alone
666	**Bhooma roopa**	She who is the aggregate of all existing things
667	**Nirdvaitha**	She who is without the sense of duality
668	**Dvaitha varjitha**	She who is beyond duality
669	**Annada**	She who gives food
670	**Vasuda**	She who gives wealth
671	**Vriddha**	She who is ancient
672	**Brahmatmaikya swaroopini**	She who merges herself with the brahman
673	**Brihathi**	She who is big
674	**Brahmani**	She who is the female aspect of Brahman
675	**Brahmi**	She who is the consort of Brahma
676	**Brahmananda**	She who is the ultimate happiness
677	**Bali priya**	She who likes sacrificial offerings
678	**Bhasha roopa**	She who is the personification of language
679	**Brihatsena**	She who has a big army
680	**Bhavabhava vivarjitha**	She who transcends birth or death

681	**Sukharadhya**	She who can be worshipped with pleasure
682	**Shubhakari**	She who makes everything auspicious
683	**Shobhana sulabha gathi**	She who is beautiful and easy to attain
684	**Raja rajeshwari**	She who is a goddess to the kings
685	**Rajya dayini**	She who gives away kingdoms
686	**Rajya vallabha**	She who protects all kingdoms
687	**Rajat krupa**	She whose compassion captivates all
688	**Raja peetha niveshitha nijashritha**	She who makes those kings who take refuge in her
689	**Rajya lakshmi**	She who is the wealth of the kingdoms
690	**Kosha nadha**	She who protects the treasures
691	**Chathuranga baleswari**	She who commands armies of four types
692	**Samrajya dayini**	She who is the bestower of empires
693	**Sathya sandha**	She who is devoted to the truth
694	**Sagara mekhala**	She who is surrounded by oceans
695	**Deekshitha**	She who is under a vow
696	**Daithya shamani**	She who suppresses the wicked forces
697	**Sarvaloka vasamkari**	She who keeps all the worlds under her control

698	**Sarvartha daatri**	She who gives all wealth
699	**Savithri**	She who is the creative power of the universe
700	**Sachidananda roopini**	She who is of the nature of existence, consciousness and bliss
701	**Deshakala parichinna**	She who is not subjected to divisions of time and space
702	**Sarvaga**	She who is everywhere and in all things
703	**Sarvamohini**	She who bewitches all
704	**Saraswathi**	She who is the goddess of knowledge
705	**Shastra mayi**	She who is the source of the shastras
706	**Guhamba**	She who abides in the cave of the heart
707	**Guhya roopini**	She whose form is hidden
708	**Sarvo padhi vinirmuktha**	She who is free from all conditions
709	**Sadashiva pativrata**	She who is a devoted wife of Shiva
710	**Sampradhaeshwari**	She who is a goddess of rituals
711	**Sadhvi**	She who is innocent and gentle
712	**Ee**	She who is the alphabet "e"
713	**Guru mandala roopini**	She who is a form of the sphere of teachers
714	**Kulotirna**	She who is beyond the senses
715	**Bhagaradhya**	She who is to be worshipped in the sun's disc

716	**Maya**	She who is illusion
717	**Madhumathi**	She whose nature is sweet as honey
718	**Mahi**	She who is the personification of earth
719	**Ganamba**	She who is mother to Shiva's attendants
720	**Guhyakaradhya**	She who is worshipped by the Guhyakas
721	**Komalangi**	She who has beautiful limbs
722	**Guru priya**	She who likes teachers
723	**Swatanthra**	She who is independent
724	**Sarva tanthreshi**	She who is a master of all tantras
725	**Dakshinamoorthi roopini**	She who is the personification of Shiva
726	**Sanakadhi samaradhya**	She who is being worshipped by Sanaka and other sages
727	**Siva jnana pradhayini**	She who gives the knowledge of Shiva
728	**Chit kala**	She who is creative consciousness
729	**Anandakalika**	She who is the source of bliss
730	**Prema roopa**	She who is the form of love
731	**Priyamkaree**	She who does what she likes
732	**Nama parayana preetha**	She who likes repetition of her various names
733	**Nandi vidya**	She who is the knowledge taught by the bull god on whom Shiva rides

734	Nateshwaree	She who is the goddess of dance
735	Mithya jaga-dadhi-shthana	She who is established in this world of illusion
736	Mukthida	She who gives redemption
737	Mukti roopini	She who is redemption
738	Lasya priya	She who likes dance
739	Laya karee	She who is the cause of musical melody
740	Lajja	She who is shy
741	Rambhadhi vandhita	She who is worshipped by the celestial dancers
742	Bhavadhava sudha vrishti	She who comforts mortal beings
743	Paparanya davanala	She who is the fire that destroys the forest of sin
744	Daurbhagya tulavathula	She who is the cyclone that blows away the strands of bad luck.
745	Jara-dhvantha ravi prabha	She who is the sunshine that swallows the darkness of old age
746	Bhagyabdhi chandrika	She who is like the full moon to the ocean of luck
747	Bhaktha chitta keki ghanagana	She who is to the devotees' mind what a dark cloud is to a peacock
748	Roga parvatha dambhola	She who is the weapon of lightning to a mountain of sickness
749	Mrutyu-daru kutharika	She who is like the axe which fells the tree of death

750	**Maheswaree**	She who is the greatest goddess
751	**Maha kali**	She who is the great Kali
752	**Maha grasa**	She who is a great devourer
753	**Mahashana**	She who is the great eater
754	**Aparna**	She who owes no debt
755	**Chandika**	She who is angry
756	**Chanda-mundasura nishudhini**	She who killed Chanda, Munda and other demons
757	**Kshara akshar-athmika**	She who is both perishable and imperishable
758	**Sarva lokeshi**	She who is the ruler of all worlds
759	**Viswa dharini**	She who supports all the universe
760	**Thrivarga dathri**	She who gives the three goals of life – dharma, prosperity and pleasure
761	**Subhaga**	She who is the giver of all auspiciousness
762	**Tryambaka**	She who has three eyes
763	**Tri-guna-athmika**	She who represents the three gunas
764	**Swargapavargada**	She who gives heaven and liberation
765	**Shuddha**	She who is clean
766	**Japapushpa nibhakrithi**	She who has the colour of hibiscus
767	**Ojovati**	She who is full of vigour
768	**Dyuthidhara**	She who is the supporter of light

769	Yagna roopa	She who is of the form of sacrifice
770	Priyavrita	She who likes penances
771	Duraradhya	She who is not easily attainable
772	Duradarsha	She who is difficult to be seen
773	Patali kusuma priya	She who likes the buds of patali tree
774	Mahati	She who is great
775	Meru nilaya	She who lives in Mount Meru
776	Mandara kusuma priya	She who likes the buds of mandhara plant
777	Veeraradhya	She who is worshipped by heroes
778	Virad roopa	She who a universal form
779	Viraja	She who does not have any impurities
780	Viswathomukhi	She who faces all directions
781	Prathyag roopa	She who can be found by looking inside oneself
782	Parakasha	She who is the great sky
783	Pranada	She who gives life breath
784	Prana roopini	She who is the form of the life breath
785	Martanda bhairava-aradhya	She who is worshipped by Martanda Bhairava
786	Mantrini nyashtha rajyadhu	She who gave Mantrini the kingdom to rule
787	Tripureshi	She who is the head of three cities

788	**Jayatsena**	She whose army always wins
789	**Nistrai gunya**	She who is free from the three qualities
790	**Parapara**	She who is transcendental and immanent
791	**Satya jnana-ananda roopa**	She who is truth, knowledge and bliss
792	**Samarasya parayana**	She who stands in peace
793	**Kapardini**	She who is the wife of Shiva
794	**Kalamala**	She who wears the arts as garlands
795	**Kamadhukh**	She who is the wish fulfilling cow
796	**Kama roopini**	She who gives shape to desires
797	**Kala nidhi**	She who is the treasure of the arts
798	**Kavya kala**	She who is the art of writing
799	**Rasajna**	She who knows all the rasas
800	**Rasa shevadhi**	She who is the treasure of rasas
801	**Pushta**	She who is healthy
802	**Puratana**	She who is ancient
803	**Pujya**	She who is worthy of worship
804	**Pushkara**	She who gives nourishment
805	**Pushkarekshana**	She who has lotus like eyes
806	**Paramjyothi**	She who is the supreme light
807	**Param dhama**	She who is the supreme abode
808	**Paramanu**	She who is the subtlest particle
809	**Parath para**	She who is better than the best

810	Pasha hastha	She who has rope in her hand
811	Pasha hanthri	She who cuts off bonds
812	Para mantra vibhedini	She who destroys the spells cast by others
813	Murtha	She who has a form
814	Amurtha	She who does not have a form
815	Anitya thriptha	She who is satisfied by our perishable offerings
816	Muni manasa hamsika	She who is the swan in the minds of sages
817	Satya vratha	She who has resolved to speak only the truth
818	Satya roopa	She who is the real form
819	Sarva-antharyamini	She who is within everything
820	Satee	She who is Satee, daughter of Daksha
821	Brahmani	She who is the strength behind the Creator
822	Brahmaa	She who is the Creator
823	Janani	She who is the mother
824	Bahuroopa	She who has several forms
825	Budharchitha	She who is being worshipped by the enlightened
826	Prasavitri	She who has given birth to everything
827	Prachanda	She who is fierce
828	Aajna	She who is the order
829	Prathishta	She who has been installed

830	**Prakata-akriti**	She who is all manifested forms
831	**Praneshwari**	She who is goddess of the senses
832	**Prana-daatri**	She who supplies the life force to the limbs in the body
833	**Panchashath peeta roopini**	She who is in fifty shakthi peethas
834	**Vishrankala**	She who is not chained
835	**Vivikthastha**	She who is found in lonely places
836	**Veera matha**	She who is the mother of heroes
837	**Viyath prasuh**	She who has created the sky
838	**Mukundaa**	She who gives redemption
839	**Mukti nilaya**	She who is the seat of redemption
840	**Mula vigraha roopini**	She who is the chief deity in a temple
841	**Bhavajna**	She who understands thoughts
842	**Bhava rokagni**	She who cures the sin of birth
843	**Bhava chakra pravarthani**	She who moves the cycle of birth and death
844	**Chanda-sara**	She who is the meaning of Vedas
845	**Shastra-sara**	She who is the essence of all scriptures
846	**Mantra-sara**	She who is the meaning of all chants
847	**Talodaree**	She who has a small belly
848	**Udara keerthi**	She whose fame is widespread
849	**Uddhhama vaibhava**	She who has unlimited prowess

850	**Varna roopini**	She who is the personification of alphabets
851	**Janma mrutyu jara tapta jana vishranti dayini**	She who is gives repose to the ills of birth, death and aging
852	**Sarvopanishadudghushta**	She who is celebrated by the Upanishads
853	**Shantyathita kalatmika**	She who is greater than peace
854	**Gambhira**	She whose depth cannot be measured
855	**Gaganantastha**	She who resides in space
856	**Garvitha**	She who is proud
857	**Gana lolupa**	She who delights in music
858	**Kalpanarahitha**	She who is free from imagined attributes
859	**Kashtha**	She who is the ultimate boundary
860	**Akantha**	She who removes sins
861	**Kantardha vigraha**	She who is the one-half of her husband
862	**Karya karana nirmuktha**	She who is beyond the action and the cause
863	**Kama keli tarangitha**	She who is overflowing with the pleasure of union with Shiva
864	**Kanat kanakatakanka**	She who wears the glittering golden ear studs
865	**Lila vigraha dharini**	She who assumes several forms as sport
866	**Aja**	She who does not have birth

867	**Kshayavinirmukta**	She who does not decay
868	**Mugdha**	She who is beautiful
869	**Kshipra prasadini**	She who is pleased quickly
870	**Antar mukha samaradhya**	She who is to be worshipped by internal thoughts
871	**Bahir mukha sudurlabha**	She who is difficult to attain by those whose attention is directed outwardly
872	**Trayee**	She who is the three Vedas
873	**Trivarga nilaya**	She who is threefold aims of human existence
874	**Tristha**	She who resides in the three worlds
875	**Tripuramalini**	She who is the goddess of Tripura
876	**Niramaya**	She who is without diseases
877	**Niralamba**	She who depends on none
878	**Swatma arama**	She who enjoys by herself
879	**Sudha shruthi**	She who is the rain of nectar
880	**Samsara panka nirmagna samuddharana panditha**	She who rescues people from the bondage of life and death
881	**Yagna priya**	She who likes fire sacrifice
882	**Yagna karthree**	She who carries out fire sacrifice
883	**Yajamana swaroopini**	She who is the doer of fire sacrifice
884	**Dharmaadhara**	She who is the basis of rightful action

885	**Dhanadyaksha**	She who presides over wealth
886	**Dhanadhanya vivardhani**	She who makes wealth and grain to grow
887	**Viprapriya**	She who likes those who learn Vedas
888	**Vipraroopa**	She who is the learner of Vedas
889	**Vishwa brahmana karini**	She who is the cause for the rotation of the universe
890	**Vishwa grasa**	She who swallows the universe
891	**Vidhrumabha**	She who has the lustre of coral
892	**Vaishnavi**	She who is the power of Vishnu
893	**Vishnu roopini**	She who is the personification of Vishnu
894	**Ayoni**	She who is without origin
895	**Yoni nilaya**	She who is the seat of creation
896	**Kutastha**	She who is stable
897	**Kula roopini**	She who is the personification of culture
898	**Veera goshti priya**	She who likes company of heroes
899	**Veera**	She who has valour
900	**Naishkarmya**	She who performs desireless actions
901	**Nadaroopini**	She who is the form of sound
902	**Vijnana kalana**	She who realizes intelligence
903	**Kalya**	She who is an expert in arts
904	**Vidagdha**	She who is an expert in everything

905	**Baindavasana**	She who sits in the bindu
906	**Tattvadhika**	She who is above all metaphysics
907	**Tattvamayee**	She who is the metaphysics
908	**Tattvamartha swaroopini**	She who is the personification of this and that
909	**Samagana priya**	She who likes the songs of the Sama veda
910	**Soumya**	She who is gentle
911	**Sadashiva kutumbini**	She who is the consort of Shiva
912	**Savyapa savya margastha**	She who stands for the right and left-hand paths
913	**Sarva apadvi nivarini**	She who removes all dangers
914	**Swastha**	She who is healthy
915	**Svabhava madhura**	She who is sweet by nature
916	**Dhira**	She who is courageous
917	**Dhira samarchida**	She who is being worshipped by the courageous
918	**Chaithnyarghya samaradhya**	She who is worshipped with consciousness as an oblation
919	**Chaitanya kusuma priya**	She who likes the flower of consciousness
920	**Sadoditha**	She who is always shining
921	**Sada thushta**	She who is always happy
922	**Tarunadithya patala**	She who like the red morning sun
923	**Dakshina dakshinaradhya**	She who is worshipped by the learned and ignorant

924	**Darasmera mukhambuja**	She who has a face like the lotus in full bloom
925	**Kaulini kevala**	She who is worshipped by followers of the kaula and kevala paths
926	**Anargya kaivalya pada dayini**	She who shows the path to liberation
927	**Stotra priya**	She who likes chants
928	**Stuthi mathi**	She who is the object of all chants
929	**Sruthi samsthutha vaibhava**	She whose glory is celebrated by the Vedas
930	**Manasvini**	She who has a stable mind
931	**Manavati**	She who is high-minded
932	**Maheshi**	She who is the greatest goddess
933	**Mangala kruthi**	She who does only good
934	**Vishwa matha**	The mother of the universe
935	**Jagat dhathri**	She who supports the world
936	**Vishalakshi**	She who is large-eyed
937	**Viragini**	She who is dispassionate
938	**Pragalbha**	She who is confident
939	**Paramodara**	She who is a great giver
940	**Paramoda**	She who has great happiness
941	**Manomayi**	She who is in the form of the mind
942	**Vyomakeshi**	She who has sky as her hair
943	**Vimanastha**	She who is at a higher realm

944	**Vajrini**	She who is Indra's wife
945	**Vamakeshwaree**	She who is goddess of the left-hand path
946	**Pancha yagna priya**	She who likes the five sacrifices
947	**Pancha pretha manchadhi shayini**	She who sleeps on the bed of five corpses
948	**Panchami**	She who is the fifth aspect of Shiva
949	**Pancha bhooteshi**	She who is the ruler of five elements air, space, fire, water and earth
950	**Pancha sankhyopacharini**	She who is to be worshipped by five substances of sandalwood, flower, incense, light of a lamp and an offering
951	**Shashvathi**	She who is permanent
952	**Shashvathaiswarya**	She who gives perennial wealth
953	**Sharmadha**	She who gives pleasure
954	**Shambhu mohini**	She who bewitches Shiva
955	**Dhara**	She who supports
956	**Dharasutha**	She who is the daughter of the mountain Mandhara
957	**Dhanya**	She who is blessed
958	**Dharmini**	She who practices dharma
959	**Dharma vardhini**	She who promotes dharma
960	**Loka theetha**	She who is beyond the world
961	**Guna theetha**	She who is beyond the properties of the cosmos
962	**Sarvatheetha**	She who is beyond everything

963	**Shamathmika**	She who is peace
964	**Bandhooka kusuma prakhya**	She who has the glitter of bandhooka flowers
965	**Bala**	She who is a young maiden
966	**Leela vinodhini**	She who enjoys play of creation
967	**Sumangali**	She who is the cause of all good things
968	**Sukha kari**	She who grants happiness
969	**Suveshadya**	She who is well-made
970	**Suvasini**	She who is sweet-scented
971	**Suvasinyarchana preetha**	She who likes the worship of married woman
972	**Shobhana**	She who is always radiant
973	**Shuddha manasa**	She who has a clean mind
974	**Bindu tarpana santhushta**	She who is happy with any offerings made to the bindu of the Sri Chakra Yantra
975	**Poorvaja**	She who is before all
976	**Tripurambika**	She who is the goddess of three cities
977	**Dasa mudra samaradhya**	She who is worshipped by ten postures of the hand
978	**Tripura sree vasankari**	She who keeps the goddess Tripura under control
979	**Jnana mudra**	She who is the symbol of knowledge
980	**Jnana gamya**	She who can be attained by knowledge
981	**Jnana gneya swaroopini**	She who embodies both knowledge and knowing

982	**Yoni mudra**	She who is the symbol of yoni
983	**Trikhandeshi**	She who is the lord of three divisions of mind, body and soul
984	**Triguna**	She who is the three qualities of sattva, tamas and rajas
985	**Amba**	She who is the mother
986	**Trikonaga**	She who stands for the vertices of a triangle
987	**Anaga**	She who is impervious to sin
988	**Adbutha charithra**	She who has a wonderful history
989	**Vanchitharta pradayini**	She who grants what is desired
990	**Abhyasa-atishaya gnatha**	She who can be realized by constant practice
991	**Shadvatheetha roopini**	She whose form transcends the six paths
992	**Avyaja karuna murty**	She who shows mercy without cause
993	**Agnana dvantha deepika**	She who is the lamp that dispels ignorance
994	**Abala gopa vidhitha**	She who is known to all from children to cowherds
995	**Sarvanullangya shasana**	She whose orders can never be disobeyed
996	**Sri chakra raja nilaya**	She who lives in the Sri Chakra
997	**Srimathtripurasundari**	The beautiful goddess
998	**Srishivaa**	She who is divine Shiva
999	**Shiva shakthaikya roopini**	She who is the unified form of Shiva and Shakti
1000	**Lalithambika**	The divine Mother Goddess

Lalita Trishati

The Lalitha Trishati is a stotra found in the Brahmanda Purana. In a chapter called Lalithopakyanam, we are told the story of how Agastya is taught the Lalitha Sahasranama by Hayagreeva but he is not entirely satisfied as he feels that something is missing in his learning. Hayagreeva insists that he has taught him all that he knows. At this point Goddess Lalitha Tripurasundari appears before Hayagreeva and instructs him to teach Agastya the Lalitha Trishati. Hayagreeva is very thankful to his disciple as he provided him an opportunity to see the Goddess and teaches him the Lalitha Trishati.

The stotra contains 300 names of the goddess which are all expansion of the Panchadasi mantra.

* Ka E I la Hrim
* Ha Sa Ka Ha La Hrim
* Sa Ka La Hrim

It begins with the *dhyana* (a description of the deity)-

"Athi madhura chapa hastha aparimitha moda bana sowbhagyam
Aruna athishaya karuna abhinava kula sundarim vande"

I bow before her

She who is red in colour

Who is mercy personified

And is an epitome of beauty

She who holds a bow made of sugarcane

And shoots arrows dispensing joy and grace

The meaning of the 300 names

1	**Kakara Roopa**	She who is like the alphabet 'ka' (represents light)
2	**Kalyani**	She who is endowed with all good qualities
3	**Kalyana guna shalini**	She who is the personification of good qualities
4	**Kalyana shaila nilaya**	She who resides at the peak of the mountain of good
5	**Kamaniya**	She who is attractive
6	**Kalavathi**	She in whom the fine arts reside (64 arts)
7	**Kamalakshi**	She who has eyes like lotus
8	**Kalmashagni**	She who destroys sin
9	**Karunamritha sagara**	She who is the sea of the nectar of compassion
10	**Kadamba kaanana vasa**	She who lives in the forest of kadamba, which is filled with Kalpa Vruksha, the tree which grants all desires
11	**Kadamba kusuma priya**	She who likes the flowers of kadamba (mind with good thoughts)
12	**Kandharpa vidya**	She who is the holy knowledge worshipped by the God of love.
13	**Kandharpa janakapanga veekshana**	She who created God of love by her sight
14	**Karpoora veedi kallolitha kakupthada**	She who fills the world with the holy scent of the betel leaf (made with ingredients like cardamom, nutmeg, mace, camphor, saffron, etc.) she chews

15	**Kali dosha hara**	She who eradicates all evils of Kaliyuga (era of Kali)
16	**Kanja lochana**	She who has eyes like lotus and takes care of the universe by her vision.
17	**Kamra vigraha**	She who has hair that can steal the mind
18	**Karmadhi sakshini**	She who is the witness for action
19	**Karayathree**	She who evokes Vedic karmas
20	**Karma phala pradha**	She who gives fruits of actions
21	**Eakara Roopa**	She who is like the alphabet 'ea' (the absolute truth)
22	**Eka ksharya**	She who is the holy word Aum
23	**Eka aneka akshara kriti**	She who is the personification of all alphabets
24	**Ethath thathithya nirdesya**	She who cannot be described as "this" or "that"
25	**Ekananda chidakriti**	She who is the personification of ultimate happiness and knowledge
26	**Evamithyaagama bodhya**	She who is beyond the scriptures
27	**Eka bhakthi madarchida**	She who is worshipped by those with single-minded devotion
28	**Ekagra chitha nirdyatha**	She who can only be meditated upon with absolute concentration
29	**Eshana rahi dathrudha**	She who is supported by those without attachment
30	**Ela sugandhi chikura**	She who has hair that smells of sweet cardamom
31	**Ena kooda vinasini**	She who destroys all sin

32	Eka bhoga	She who is the object of enjoyment
33	Eka rasa	She who is the essence of the only love
34	Ekaiswarya pradayini	She who gives the real and only asset - the asset of salvation
35	Ekatha pathra samrajya pradha	She who gives one the power to be the emperor of the world
36	Ekanda poojitha	She who can be worshipped in absolute solitude
37	Edhamana prabha	She who has the greatest lustre
38	Ejadeneka jagadeeswari	She who is the goddess of all the moving worlds
39	Eka veeradhi samsevya	She who is worshipped by the brave warriors first
40	Eka prabhava shalini	She who is the only brilliant power
41	Eekara Roopa	She who is like the alphabet "ee" (that makes us all move)
42	Eesithri	She who is the motivating force behind everything
43	Eepsithartha pradayini	She who gives us what we ask for
44	Eedrigithya vi nirdesya	She who cannot be limited or described by word "like this"
45	Eeswaratwa vidhayini	She who establishes oneness with Eshwara, thereby destroying duality
46	Eesanadhi brahma mayi	She who the embodiment of 5 gods
47	Eesithwadh ashta siddhidha	She who gives the eight supernatural powers

48	**Eekshithri**	She who exists because of her will
49	**Eekshana srushtanda kotya**	She who creates billions of beings by her will
50	**Eeswara vallabha**	She who is the consort of Lord Shiva
51	**Eeditha**	She who is praised in the Vedas and Puranas
52	**Eeswarardhanga sareera**	She who is half the body of Shiva
53	**Eesaadhi devatha**	She who is the Goddess to Shiva
54	**Eeswara prerana kari**	She who motivates Shiva to create
55	**Eesa thandava sakshini**	She who is the witness to the cosmic dance of Shiva
56	**Eeswaroth sanga nilaya**	She who sits on the lap of Shiva
57	**Eedhi badhaa vinashini**	She who stops unexpected calamities
58	**Eeha virahitha**	She who is free from all desires
59	**Eesha shakthi**	She who is the power within Shiva
60	**Eeshath smithanana**	She who has a smiling face
61	**Lakara roopa**	She who is the form of alphabet "la" (the wave which initiates wisdom)
62	**Lalitha**	She who is like the mother who plays with her children
63	**Lakshmi vani nishevitha**	She who is served by Lakshmi, the goddess of wealth and Sarawathi, the goddess of knowledge
64	**Laakhini**	She who is easily approachable

65	**Lalana roopa**	She who has a female form
66	**Lasadh dhardima paatala**	She who is the colour of pomegranate flower in bloom
67	**Lalanthika lasadh bala**	She who wears a beautiful thilaka made of precious gems
68	**Lalada nayanarchidha**	She who is worshipped by yogis with insight
69	**Lakshanojwala divyangi**	She who shines with all divine qualities
70	**Laksha kodyanda nayika**	She who is the lord of billions of universes
71	**Lakshyartha**	She who is the meaning of all Vedanta
72	**Lakshanagamya**	She who cannot be understood by explanations
73	**Labdhakama**	She who has achieved all desires
74	**Lathathanu**	She whose body is ever young like a tendril
75	**Lalamara jadhalika**	She who wears a thilaka made of musk
76	**Lambi muktha lathanchitha**	She who beautifies herself with a necklace made of pearls
77	**Lambodhara prasa**	She who is the mother of Lord Ganapati
78	**Labhya**	She who can be attained by contemplation and meditation
79	**Lajjadya**	She who has the wealth of shyness
80	**Laya varjitha**	She who is free from destruction

81	**Hreemgara Roopa**	She who is of the form of word "hreem" (denoting creation, preservation and destruction)
82	**Hreemgara nilaya**	She who resides in hreem
83	**Hreem pada priya**	She who likes the manthra hreem
84	**Hreem kara beejha**	She who is identified by the manthra "hreem"
85	**Hreem kara manthra**	She who has hreem as manthra
86	**Hreem kara lakshana**	She who has hreem as an attribute
87	**Hreemkara japa supreetha**	She who is pleased by the recitation of hreem
88	**Hreemathi**	She who is represented by hreem
89	**Hreemvibhushana**	She who has hreem as an ornament
90	**Hreem shila**	She who has all the good qualities of hreem
91	**Hreem padaradhya**	She who can be worshipped by the word hreem
92	**Hreem garbha**	She who carries hreem in her womb
93	**Hreem padhabidha**	She who takes the name of hreem
94	**Hreemkara vachya**	She who is referred to as hreem
95	**Hreemkara poojya**	She who is worshipped by hreem
96	**Hreem kara peediga**	She who is the basis of hreem
97	**Hreemkara vedhya**	She who can be realized by hreem
98	**Hreemkara chinthya**	She who can be meditated on through hreem

99	**Hreem**	She who gives the ultimate bliss
100	**Hreem sareerini**	She who has her body as hreem
101	**Hakara roopa**	She who is of the form of alphabet "ha" (the valour to kill enemies)
102	**Hala drith poojitha**	She who is worshipped by the one with the plough
103	**Harinekshana**	She who has eyes like a doe
104	**Harapriya**	She who is the beloved of Vishnu
105	**Hararadhya**	She who is worshipped by Shiva
106	**Haribrahmendra vanditha**	She who is worshipped by Brahma, Vishnu and Indra
107	**Haya roodaa sevithangri**	She whose feet are taken care of by Indra
108	**Hayamedha samarchidha**	She who is worshipped during Ashwa medha yagna
109	**Haryaksha vahana**	She who rides the lion in the form of Durga
110	**Hamsa vahana**	She who rides the swan in the form of Saraswathi
111	**Hatha dhanava**	She who kills asuras
112	**Hathyadi papa samani**	She who reduces the effect of sins
113	**Harid aswadhi sewitha**	She who is worshipped by Indra
114	**Hasthi kumbhothunga kucha**	She who has breasts as high as the forehead of the elephant
115	**Haathi krithi priyangana**	She who is the darling of Shiva who wears elephant skin

116	**Haridhra kumkuma digdha**	She whose body is covered with turmeric and kumkum (saffron)
117	**Haryaswadhya amara archidha**	She who is worshiped by Indra and other devas
118	**Harikesa sakhi**	She who is the friend of Paramasiva
119	**Hadhi vidhya**	She who is the personification of Hadhi vidhya
120	**Halaa madhalasa**	She who is drunk on wine which was created from the ocean of milk
121	**Sakara roopa**	She who is of the form of alphabet "sa" (material wealth and pleasures)
122	**Sar vagna**	She who knows everything
123	**Sarvesi**	She who stimulates everything
124	**Sarva mangala**	She who is auspicious by nature
125	**Sarva karthri**	She who is the "doer" of all actions
126	**Sarva bharthri**	She who takes care of everything
127	**Sarva hanthri**	She who destroys everything
128	**Sanathani**	She who does not have a beginning or an end
129	**Sarva navadhya**	She who does not have any blemish
130	**Sarvanga sundari**	She who embodies beauty
131	**Sarva sakshini**	She who is the witness of everything
132	**Sarvathmika**	She who is the soul of everything
133	**Sarva sowkhya dhatri**	She who gives all kinds of happiness
134	**Sarva vimohini**	She who enchants
135	**Sarvadhara**	She who is the basis of everything
136	**Sarva gatha**	She who is omniscient

137	**Sarva avaguna varjitha**	She who is free of all bad qualities
138	**Sarvaruna**	She who is red in colour and is the dawn of everything
139	**Sarva maatha**	She who is the mother of creation
140	**Sarva bhooshana bhooshitha**	She who has worn all ornaments
141	**Kakara artha**	She whose meaning is the alphabet 'ka' (represents light)
142	**Kala hanthri**	She who is the destroyer of time
143	**Kameshi**	She who evokes desires
144	**Kamithartha da**	She who fulfills all desires
145	**Kama sanjivini**	She who brought the God of love to life
146	**Kalya**	She who is fit to be meditated upon
147	**Kadina sthana mandala**	She who has firm breasts
148	**Kara bhoru**	She who has thighs like the elephant's trunk
149	**Kala nadha mukhya**	She who has a face like a full moon
150	**Kacha jitambudha**	She who has hair like dark clouds
151	**Kadakshyandhin karuna**	She who has a merciful vision
152	**Kapali prana nayiga**	She who is the wife of Shiva
153	**Karunya vigraha**	She who personifies mercy
154	**Kantha**	She who is the stealer of minds
155	**Kanthi dhootha japavali**	She who has lustre more than flowers have

156	**Kalalapa**	She whose speech sounds like music
157	**Kambhu kanti**	She who has a conch-like neck
158	**Kara nirjitha pallava**	She whose hands are softer than tender buds
159	**Kalpa valli sama bhuja**	She who has arms as beautiful as the kalpaga creeper
160	**Kasturi thilakanchitha**	She who wears thilaka with musk
161	**Hakarartha**	She whose meaning is the alphabet 'ha' (money, valour)
162	**Hamsa gathi**	She whose gait is like a swan
163	**Haataka abharnojjwala**	She who shines wearing gold ornaments
164	**Haara Haari kucha bhoga**	She who has a breast decorated by ornaments
165	**Hakini**	She who cuts bounds of life and death
166	**Halya varjitha**	She who is free from deceptions
167	**Harithpathi samaradhya**	She who is being worshipped by the eight gods who guard the different directions
168	**Hatahthkara hathasura**	She who killed the asuras with her bravery
169	**Harsha pradha**	She who gives happiness
170	**Havirbhokthri**	She who partakes the offering given to devas in fire
171	**Hardha santhama sapaha**	She who removes darkness from the mind
172	**Halleesa lasya santhushta**	She who is pleased with the dance of girls

173	**Hamsa manthrartha roopini**	She who understands the meaning of the manthra relating to breath control
174	**Hanopadhana nirmuktha**	She who is beyond wants
175	**Harshini**	She who blesses one with happiness
176	**Hari shodari**	She who is the sister of Lord Vishnu
177	**Haahaa hoohoo mukha sthutya**	She who is being praised by Gandharvas called Haahaa and Hoohoo
178	**Hani vriddhi vivarjitha**	She who has got beyond growth and stagnation
179	**Hayyangavina hridhaya**	She who has a heart like butter
180	**Harikoparunam shuka**	She who is dressed in red
181	**Lakarakhya**	She whose meaning is the alphabet 'la'
182	**Latha poojya**	She who is worshipped by chaste women
183	**Laya sthith udbhaveswari**	She who is the supreme Goddess
184	**Lasya darshana santhushta**	She who gets pleased by seeing women dancing
185	**Labha labha vivarjitha**	She who is beyond loss and gain
186	**Langye tharagna**	She who gives orders which cannot be disobeyed
187	**Lavanya shalini**	She who is of unmatched beauty and grace

188	**Laghu siddhita**	She who gives supernatural powers easily
189	**Laksha rasa savarnabha**	She who shines like lac
190	**Lakshmanagraja poojitha**	She who was worshipped by Rama
191	**Labhyethara**	She who can help acquire dharma, artha, kama and moksha
192	**Labdha bhakthi sulabha**	She who can be attained by devotion
193	**Langalayudha**	She who has a plough as a weapon
194	**Lagna chamara hastha sri sharadha parivijitha**	She who is served by Lakshmi and Saraswathi (actually fanned by them)
195	**Lajjapada samaradhya**	She who is the most fit to be worshipped by those who shun this world
196	**Lampata**	She who has hidden herself from the earthly principles
197	**Lakuleshwari**	She in whom the entire world merges together
198	**Labdha maana**	She who is praised by all
199	**Labdha rasa**	She whose nature is ultimate happiness
200	**Labdha sampath samunnadhi**	She who has attained the apex of riches
201	**Hrimkarini**	She who is the personification of the letter "Hrim"
202	**Hrimkaradhi**	She who is the origin of hrim and Om
203	**Hrim Madhya**	She who is in the midst of hrim

204	**Hrim Shikhamani**	She who wears hrim on her head as an ornament
205	**Hrim kara kundagni shikha**	She who is the flame of the fire place called hrim
206	**Hrim kara shasi chandrika**	She who is the nectar like rays of the moonlight called hrim
207	**Hrimkara bhaskara ruchi**	She who is the powerful rays of the sun called hrim
208	**Hrimkarambodha chanchala**	She who is the lightning in the black clouds called hrim
209	**Hrimkara kandham kurika**	She who is the germinating tendril of the tuber called hrim
210	**Hrimkaraiga parayana**	She who reminds us of hrim
211	**Hrim kara deergiga hamsi**	She who is the swan playing in the pond called hrim
212	**Hrimkarodhyana kekini**	She who is the peahen playing in the garden of hrim
213	**Hrimkararanya harini**	She who is the doe playing in the forest of hrim
214	**Hrimkaravaala vallari**	She who is the ornamental climber in the flower bed of hrim
215	**Hrim kara panchara sukhi**	She who is the green parrot in the cage called hrim
216	**Hrimkarangana deepika**	She who is the light kept in the courtyard called hrim
217	**Hrimkara kandhara simhi**	She who is the lioness living in the cave called hrim
218	**Hrimkarambhoja bringika**	She who is the bee playing in the lotus called hrim

219	Hrimkara sumano maadhvi	She who is the honey in the flower called hrim
220	Hrimkara tharu manjari	She who is the flower in the tree called hrim
221	Sakarakhya	She who is of the form of alphabet "sa"
222	Samarasa	She who is uniformly spread in the universe
223	Sakalagama samsthitha	She who is being praised by all kinds of worship
224	Sarva vedantha thatparya bhoomi	She who is the basis of Vedanta
225	Sad asada ashraya	She who is a refuge for the formless
226	Sakhala	She who is complete
227	Satchidananda	She who is the ultimate bliss
228	Saadhya	She who is reachable by devotees
229	Sadgathi Dhayini	She who gives salvation
230	Sanakathi muni dhyeyi	She who is being meditated upon by sages like Sanaka
231	Sada shiva kudumbini	She who is the wife of Sada Shiva
232	Sakaladhishtana roopa	She who is the basis of all establishments
233	Sathya roopa	She who is the personification of truth
234	Samaa krithi	She who treats everybody equally
235	Sarva prapancha nirmathri	She who has made the universe

236	**Samanadhika varjitha**	She who is incomparable
237	**Sarvothunga**	She who is the greatest among all
238	**Sanga hina**	She who does not have attachments
239	**Saguna**	She who has all the good qualities
240	**Sakaleshtada**	She who gives all that is desired
241	**Kakarini**	She who sounds like the alphabet "ka"
242	**Kavya lola**	She who enjoys poetry
243	**Kameshwara manohara**	She who steals the mind of Shiva
244	**Kameswara prana nadi**	She who is the ultimate influencer of the soul of Shiva
245	**Kameshoth sanga vasini**	She who sits on the left lap of Shiva
246	**Kameshawara alingathangi**	She who is embraced by Shiva
247	**Kameshwara sukha pradha**	She who gives pleasure to Shiva
248	**Kameshwara pranayini**	She who is the love of Shiva
249	**Kameshwara vilasini**	She who pleases Shiva
250	**Kameshwara thapa siddhi**	She who is the result of penance done by Shiva
251	**Kameshwara mana priya**	She who is most dear to Shiva
252	**Kameshwara prana nadha**	She who is the ruler of the mind of the god of Kama (the god of love)

253	**Kameshwara vimohini**	She who steals the mind of Shiva
254	**Kameshwara brahma vidya**	She who is the science of reaching the truth as revealed by Shiva
255	**Kameshwara griheswari**	She who is the goddess of the entire universe
256	**Kameshwara ahladhakaree**	She who makes Shiva supremely happy
257	**Kameshwara maheswari**	She who is the supreme goddess of Shiva
258	**Kameshwari**	She who is being worshipped by Shiva
259	**Kama koti nilaya**	She who presides over the Kama koti peeta
260	**Kamakshitharthada**	She who fulfils the desires of devotees
261	**Lakarini**	She who sounds like the alphabet "la"
262	**Labdha roopa**	She who has taken a form with all good qualities
263	**Labhdha di**	She who has knowledge of all things
264	**Labhdha vanchitha**	She who has all that she desires
265	**Labhdha papa mano dhoora**	She who is far from the reach of sinners
266	**Labhdha ahankara dhurghama**	She whom people with ego will find difficult to reach
267	**Labhdha shakthi**	She who gets all the powers by her will
268	**Labhdha deha**	She who gets a body if she wills
269	**Labdha iswarya samunnathi**	She who can get wealth by her will

270	**Labhdha vriddhi**	She who has reached the infinite
271	**Labhdha leela**	She who can make others happy with her playfulness
272	**Labhdha yovana shalini**	She who is forever young by her will
273	**Labhdahika sarvanga soundarya**	She who is the supreme beauty by her will
274	**Labhdha vibrama**	She who echants by her playfulness
275	**Labhdha raga**	She who has all the feelings
276	**Labhdha pathi**	She who has Shiva as her husband
277	**Labhdha nanagama sthithi**	She who leads to the existence of scriptures
278	**Labhdha bhoga**	She who has all kinds of pleasures
279	**Labhdha sukha**	She who enjoys comforts
280	**Labhdha harshabhi pooritha**	She who is the refuge of all happiness
281	**Hrimkara moorthi**	She who is the personification of hrim
282	**Hrim kara soudha shringa kaphodhiga**	She who is the dove who lives in the palace called hrim
283	**Hrim kara durghabdhi sudha**	She who is the nectar churned out from the ocean of milk called hrim
284	**Hrimkara kamalendhira**	She who is Goddess Lakshmi sitting on the lotus called hrim
285	**Hrimkara mani deeparchi**	She who is the light of the ornamental lamp called hrim
286	**Hrimkara tharu sharika**	She who is the bird sitting on the tree called hrim

287	**Hrimkara petaka mani**	She who is the pearl locked in a shell called hrim
288	**Hrimkaradarsha bimbhidha**	She who is the image reflected in the mirror called hrim
289	**Hrimkara koshashilatha**	She who is the shining sword in the sheath called hrim
290	**Hrimkara sthana narthaki**	She who is the dancer on a stage called hrim
291	**Hrimkara shukthika mukthamani**	She who is the pearl found in the oyster shell called hrim
292	**Hrimkara bodhitha**	She is hrim and hrim is She
293	**Hrimkaramaya sowarna stambha vidhruma puthrika**	She who is the coral statue on the shining pillars called hrim
294	**Hrimkara vedhoupanishad**	She who is the Upanishad placed in the top in Vedas called hrim
295	**Hrimkara dwara dakshina**	She who is the dakshina gifted to priests after they complete a yagna called hrim
296	**Hrimkara nandhanarama nava kalpaga vallari**	She who is the new divine climber present in the garden called hrim
297	**Hrimkara himavath ganga**	She who is the river Ganga in the Himalaya mountain called hrim
298	**Hrimkararnava kousthubha**	She who is the precious gem arising from the ocean called hrim
299	**Hrimkara manthra sarvasva**	She who is the total wealth churned out of the manthra "hrim"
300	**Hrimkarapara sowkhyadha**	She who gives all pleasures to those who chant "hrim"

6
MUDRAS FOR RELAXATION

In the Yogic tradition, a great deal of emphasis is placed on the position and movement of hands during the practice of asana and meditation. These hand gestures are known as mudras.

The word mudra is derived from the Sanskrit word "mudh" which means "lock or seal." The deliberate positioning of fingers and hands helps direct or seal energy flow, thereby allowing the prana or life force to move freely to rejuvenate and heal the body. While foot reflexology has gained much popularity in modern times, it must not be forgotten that the fingers and hands also have more than four thousand nerve endings corresponding to various organs and functions of the body. Various parts of the brain can be stimulated by applying pressure to the finger tips or by curling and pointing the fingers in specified directions.

Although mudras are used extensively by practitioners of yoga, meditation and dance, they can also be a very useful practice in everyday life to optimize health and wellbeing and bring about a state of peace and harmony. Yoga texts feature hundreds of mudras, which range from specific healing modalities for particular ailments to ones that promote a feeling of general wellbeing and relaxation. In this chapter, I am focusing on some mudras which help bring about relief from stress and anxiety.

How to practice mudras

* You can practice mudras at any time of the day or night.
* Find a quiet space where you can sit without distraction for about 20 minutes each day.
* It would be ideal if you could sit in Padmasana, Sukhasana or Vajrasana, with spine erect and shoulders relaxed.
* It is better to use both hands while doing the mudras to enhance their effect.
* You can hold each mudra for about 12 to 15 breaths and then move on to the next one.
* Move the fingers and hands effortlessly from one mudra to another to resemble a flow.
* Pay attention to the breath and observe how it slows down as the body becomes more and more relaxed with every mudra practiced.

Mudras for relaxation and stress management

You can start with the namaskara mudra. Bring both the palms together and feel the energies circulate through the hands. This mudra represents the interconnectedness of all things in the universe. Beginning with this gesture is a way to honour yourself and your role in the larger scheme of life.

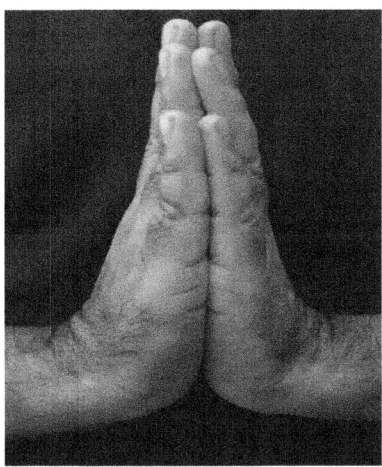

Namaskara mudra

Move into gyana mudra. With the palms facing upwards, press the tip of the index finger to the tip of the thumb. Try to keep the other three fingers straight. This commonly used mudra increases focus and helps bring about deep relaxation. You may rest the palm on the thigh if you wish to feel more grounded.

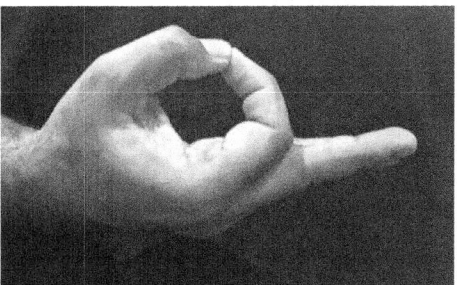

Gyana mudra

Gently reposition the fingers into the Shuni mudra. Bring the tip of the middle finger and thumb together applying gentle pressure. This mudra helps in bringing about a sense of stability, enhancing patience and calm. This mudra can be especially useful when you feel overwhelmed. It helps build resilience and supports in completing unfinished tasks.

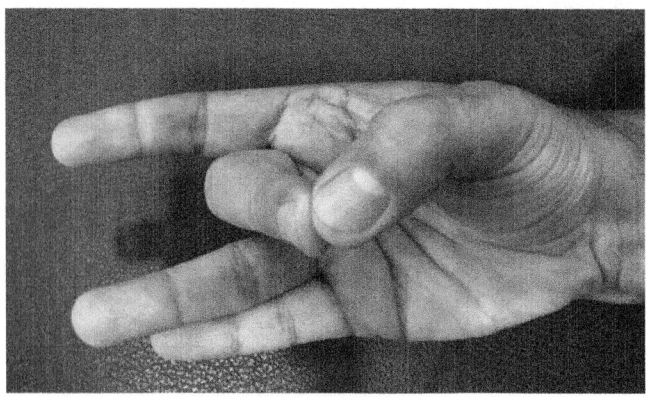

Shuni mudra

Move the fingers seamlessly into the prana mudra. This mudra activates prana which may be lying dormant in the body. Bring the tips of the thumb, ring finger and little finger together while keeping the other two fingers erect. This mudra encourages the flow of prana, making you feel energized and rejuvenated.

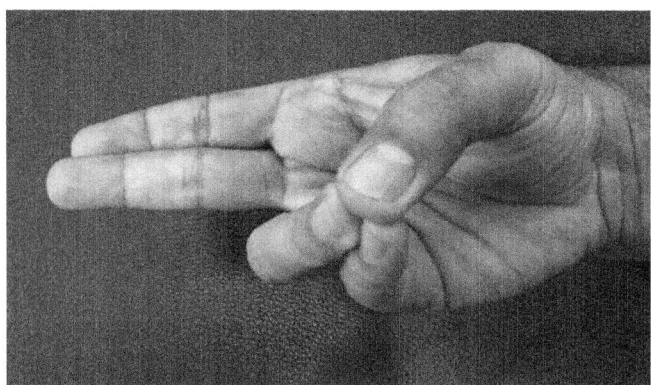

Prana mudra

Bring the hands into the lap for the dhyana mudra. With the palms facing upwards, keep the left palm below the right one and touch the tips of the thumbs. This mudra brings about a calming energy and is typically used during meditation as it enhances contemplation and inner growth.

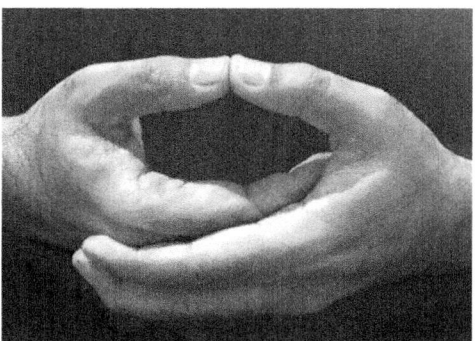

Dhyana mudra

Slowly join the little fingers and ring fingers of both hands. Fold the middle and index fingers loosely over the thumb. Bend the thumb towards the palms. This is the Shakti Mudra. This mudra promotes sound sleep and brings about deep relaxation. It is highly recommended for those suffering from insomnia or anxiety attacks.

Shakti mudra

Gently stretch out and place the index fingers against each other and let the other fingers and thumbs rest, interlocking each other. Point the index finger downwards while holding the hands in front of the chest. This is the powerful Kshepana mudra, whose main function is to draw out all the negative energies from your body and to help let go of all emotions which are no longer necessary to the wellbeing.

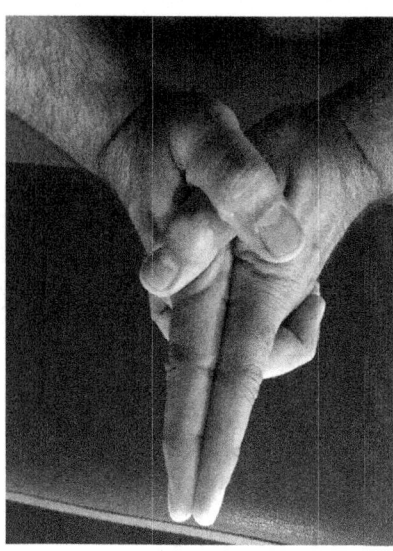

Kshepana mudra

Interlock all the fingers and keep the index fingers and thumbs pointing outward. Place the hands just above the navel and point the index fingers upwards and thumbs downward. This is the Uttara bodhi mudra, often termed as the mudra of enlightenment. It helps dissipate fears, anxiety and phobias and can be particularly useful before an interview, examination or in stressful or traumatic times.

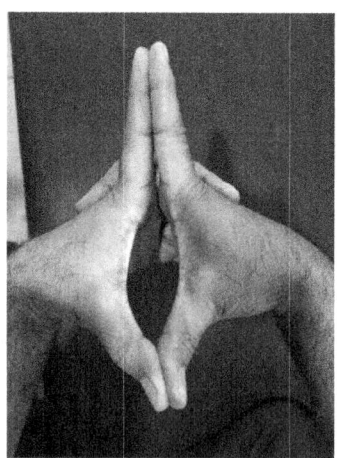

Uttara Bodhi mudra

The above mudras can be safely practiced during pregnancy, lactation and while recovering from serious illness or trauma.

Mudras require no special equipment and can be performed at any time or place. You can practice them while commuting or travelling, at your desk or even while watching over your children in a park. Remember to focus on healing yourself from within when you are practicing. Regular practice of these mudras will help you become calmer and less impulsive and prone to anger and anxiety. You can use the power of the ancient science of mudras to help heal any specific ailment that you may be suffering from or just practice them to prevent illness and promote a better sense of wellbeing.

Mudras of the Sri Chakra

I do not recommend learning the Sri Chakra mudras without the supervision of a guru.

However, just to give you a glimpse into the subject, the mudras are explained below.

Each avarana of the Sri Chakra has a mudra that represents its specific energies. These mudras are used by practitioners when they perform the long, ritualistic Navavarna Puja. But they can be practiced to further strengthen the meditation on the Sri Chakra.

Avaranas and corresponding mudras

Trilokya Mohana Chakra	Sarva Samkshobini Mudra
Sarvasa Paripuraka Chakra	Sarva Vidravini Mudra
Sarva Samkshobana Chakra	Sarvakarshini Mudra
Sarva Saubhagyadayaka Chakra	Sarva Vasamkari Mudra
Sarvartha Sadhaka Chakra	Sarvon Madhini Mudra
Sarva Rakshakara Chakra	Sarva Mahankusha Mudra
Sarva Rogahara Chakra	Sarva Khechari Mudra
Sarva Siddhi Prada Chakra	Sarva Beeja Mudra
Sarvananda Maya Chakra	Sarva Yoni Mudra

How to do the mudras

Sarva Samkshobini Mudra – Raise both the index fingers and keep all the other fingertips together

Sarva Vidravini Mudra – Raise the index and middle fingers and keep other fingertips together

Sarvakarshini Mudra – Raise the index and middle fingers and keep other finger tips together. Now bend the index and middle fingers keeping all other fingertips together

Sarva Vasamkari Mudra – Open both the palms and interlock all the fingers. Make a fist keeping the thumbs inside

Sarvon Madhini Mudra – Hold the little finger of the right hand with the little finger of the left hand. Hold the little finger of the left hand with the right hand middle finger. Press middle fingers using thumbs while keeping the ring and index fingers straight.

Sarva Mahankusha Mudra – Hold the little finger of the right hand with the little finger of the left hand. Hold the little finger of the left hand with the right hand middle finger. Press middle fingers using while keeping ring and index fingers straight. Now bend the index fingers.

Sarva Khechari Mudra – Fold the middle and little fingers inward and insert the ring finger behind the middle finger and catch the tip of the ring finger with the index finger. Straighten the little and middle fingers and keep the tips together while pressing the thumb on to the top line of the middle finger. Now place the left elbow on the right elbow and rotate the wrist to have the left wrist behind the right one.

Sarva Beeja Mudra –	Catch the right hand little finger with left hand little finger and at the same time, catch the left hand little finger with the right hand ring finger. Make a round shape using the thumb and index fingers and keep the middle finger pointing straight up.
Sarva Yoni Mudra –	Fold the middle and little fingers inward and insert the ring finger behind the middle finger and catch the tip of the the ring finger with the index finger. Straighten the little and middle fingers and keep the tips together while pressing the thumb on to the top line of the middle finger.

7
SATTVIC LIFESTYLE FOR THE SRI CHAKRA YANTRA PRACTITIONER

"Sattva Guna, being pure, is illuminating, and it frees one from all reactions of bad karma. Those situated in that mode become conditioned by a sense of happiness and knowledge."

– Bhagawat Gita

In Hindu philosophy, all matter arises from Prakriti, the fundamental substance of the universe. From Prakriti arise the five Panchabhutas (elements – space, earth, fire, water and air) and three gunas (qualities). These constitute the whole of nature (energy, matter and consciousness) that pervade all objects and beings in relative amounts.

The three gunas are sattva (pure essence), rajas (activity) and tamas (inertia). Each of these gunas are present in our mind, body and spirit.

Sattva is the most superior of all gunas. In the universe, it is Sattva that is responsible for creation. Sattva is the quality of intelligence, virtue and goodness. It creates balance, harmony and stability. It is light (as opposed to heavy) and light-giving (luminous) in nature. Sattva possesses an inward and upward motion and is responsible for bringing about the awakening of the soul. It provides happiness and contentment of a lasting nature. It is the principle of clarity, wideness and peace, and the force of love that unites all things.

A sattvic person has mental clarity and is pure in thoughts, words and actions.

If an analogy were to be made with an animal, Sattva would be an elephant - intelligent, strong and gentle.

Rajas denotes activity. In cosmic terms, Rajas is responsible for maintenance and nurturing of what has already been created. Rajas is the quality of movement, change and turbulence. Rajas possesses a chaotic movement in all directions with no fixed actions. It is very helpful in offering motivation, giving shape to dreams and acting as a call to action.

A Rajasic person has a restless and highly active mind that is always seeking to be involved in activity and is focussed on material achievement and social progress.

A good example of rajasic nature would be that of a tiger's - who is fierce, aggressive, strong and restless and always on the move.

Tamas stands for inertia. In the context of the universe, Tamas denotes destruction. Tamas is the quality of darkness (as opposed to light), dullness and non-activity. It possesses a downward motion that causes decay and disintegration. It helps us by giving us the ability to complete the tasks that are initiated by Sattva and Rajas.

A tamasic person is slow, bulky and lethargic and most likely to be depressed and ungrateful.

In the animal kingdom, a good example of tamas would be a jackal. Lazy, brooding and cunning, the jackal finds ways of reducing its work by feeding on other animal's leftovers.

As humans, we have the unique opportunity to consciously influence the three gunas in our minds and bodies. Even though we cannot separate or fully eliminate one or the other of these gunas, we can choose to increase or decrease the relative amount of each one by our conscious actions. The concept of swasthya (good health) in Ayurveda highlights the importance of leading a sattvic or balanced life. In our lives, most situations are tamastic or rajasic in nature. Sattva is the result of harmonizing these skilfully and maintaining a balance.

A balanced personality is a combination of all gunas in different measures but the most positive and content personality displays more sattvic qualities. We are told repeatedly in the Vedas that our basic nature is satchitananda (ever blissful). As a result of our interactions with the external world, we sometimes become disconnected from the silent and peaceful source of our *Atma* due to an imbalance of the gunas.

It is possible to bring more sattva in our lives by making conscious and mindful choices about all that we come into contact with by focussing on making alterations in two aspects of our daily lives:

* *Aahara* or diet
* *Vihara* or lifestyle.

Aahara

"By changing dietary habits the human organism may be cured without using any medicine, while with hundreds of good medicines, diseases of the human organism cannot be cured if the food is wrong. Right food is the only key to good health."

– *Sushruta Samhita*

Health is a state of harmonious chemical balance in a living organism. Our health depends on the chemical environments inside and outside of our bodies. Food plays an important role in creating the internal chemical environment. Food, when cooked properly, is appetizing, flavourful and aromatic. Food that is cooked with love, guided by knowledge of the ingredients and served in an inspiring atmosphere becomes healing.

Ayurvedic texts emphasize that "ahara" or proper diet is very important to promote health and happiness. Food creates health by enlivening the body's inner intelligence to create harmony. When we eat foods that are right for us, we provide balance to each cell, thereby ensuring optimum functioning of all the organs.

Western nutritionists have propound theories which are meant to be common to people of all ages and medical conditions. In Ayurveda, it is believed that there is no single diet or food that is healthy for all individuals. It is only by following a diet prescribed for our particular constitution that we will lead ourselves to a state of good health.

Vegetarian food cooked with healing herbs and energizing spices can eliminate many toxins that enter the body through polluted water and air and even noise. Toxins can also enter our bodies through radiation or chemicals that are supposed to prevent our food from decay and that are used freely on vegetables, fruits and all types of edible food. Spices - concentrated " chemicals" that are converted into cleansing and vitalizing frequencies by our electrochemical system - save our body from chemical imbalance.

All the food that we eat have a chemical nature. Although these foods may contain many different chemicals, they produce only six different tastes. Ayurveda, therefore, categorizes all the food items as having one of the six tastes:

Sweet

Sour

Salty

Bitter

Pungent

Astringent

Each of these tastes is a combination of two of the five elements: earth, water, fire, air and akasha. These tastes are directly responsible for the operation and balance among the three doshas: Vata, Pitta and Kapha. Each of these tastes have special health giving properties and are beneficial if they are administered in proper dosages.

An Ayurvedic meal should provide all the six tastes in one meal. Unless all these tastes are consumed in turn, some taste buds will remain unsatisfied and the system will experience a chemical deficiency. A balanced meal should include all the tastes - some in large quantities and some in smaller, according to their potencies.

These 6 tastes affect the doshas as well. Different food items cause specific doshas to increase or decrease. Doshas increase and decrease on the principle of "like attracts like." If our prakruti is predominantly pitta, we will show a marked preference for food that tends to aggravate pitta. Food that decreases a particular dosha is said to pacify the dosha, while those that increase the dosha are said to aggravate it.

Foods for various constitutions

	Vata	**Pitta**	**Kapha**
Taste	Sweet, sour, salty	Sweet, bitter and astringent	Bitter, pungent and astringent
Grains	Rice, oats, wheat	Barley, rice, wheat	Buckwheat, millet
Vegetables	Cooked well	Cooked or raw	Raw vegetables
	Carrots, sweet potatoes, celery, leafy greens, cabbage, cucumber	Cauliflower, mushrooms, beans, okra, potatoes, sprouts, leafy greens	All vegetables except potatoes, tomatoes and cucumber
Fruits	Bananas, dates, figs, mangoes, melons, papaya, pineapple, plum	All sweet fruits but avoid sour and very juicy fruits. Apples, dried fruits, oranges, melons, pomegranates	Avoid very sweet and very sour fruits. Dried fruits are the best. Apples, apricots, mangoes, peaches and pears

Meat	Vata types need flesh foods. Eggs, goat, chicken and fish may be consumed	Avoid seafood and all flesh foods as they encourage aggression and irritability	Kapha types rarely need flesh food. If they do eat, the meat must be roasted or baked, never fried.
Nuts and seeds	Almonds	Coconut	Avoid nuts and seeds
Oils	Sesame	Almond, coconut and olive oil	Sunflower oil is best
Dairy Products	All dairy products	All sweet dairy products	Small amounts of ghee, milk
Sweeteners	Sweet reduces Vata, so sweets are recommended in moderate form	Pitta is relieved by sweet, so sweets may be consumed in moderation	Kapha is increased by sweet, so avoid all sweets
Spices	Garlic, ginger	Cardamom, cinnamon, fennel, turmeric, small amounts of cumin and black pepper	Can use all spices except excessive salt.

Some tips on the following sattvic diet

* Seek foods that are rich in *Prana* (life force). Pick foods that are organic, fresh, in season and locally produced as they are nutritionally the richest and carry the strongest, vital energy.
* As far as possible, stick to eating vegetarian food. Fresh vegetables, fruits, whole grains, lentils, nuts and spices enhance Sattva.
* Adopt a diet that consists of food which suit your prakruti

- Consume food when it is warm as the warmth stimulates the digestive enzymes and facilitates digestion. Avoid excessively dry food.

- Allow at least 6 hours between each meal. Ensure that the previous meal is completely digested.

- Avoid food which has been refrigerated or microwaved as they tend to lose prana. Keep away from processed, artificially coloured, canned and chemically preserved foods as they increase *ama* or toxic undigested matter in the body.

- Ghee (clarified butter) is one of Ayurveda's most treasured food items as it plays a key role in balancing hormones and maintaining healthy cholesterol as it contains omega-3 fatty acids. Ghee has a high heat point, which prevents it from producing free radicals that damage cell function. Incorporate ghee in your diet in moderate quantities without guilt.

- Eat foods which are high in fibre and complex carbohydrates. These foods provide lasting energy throughout the day. Fibre also helps maintain a toned digestive tract by providing bulk, which helps in evacuating toxins and excesses. When the intestines are regularly cleaned, the body does not become overloaded with digested material that would otherwise seek elimination through the skin.

- Avoid consuming excess amounts of salt as it leads to water retention and elevates blood pressure. Use pink Himalayan rock salt or lime juice to add flavour if non-salted food seem unpalatable.

- Avoid refined sugars which provide empty calories. Refined carbohydrates give the body a quick boost of energy but puts considerable stress on the pancreas and adrenals, devitalizing the body. Refined carbohydrates deplete the body of minerals, which are so important for all vital functions.

- Ensure that you get the right amount of proteins. It is better to eat vegetables which are rich in proteins. Diets high in animal proteins increase the toxicity of waste products in the body due to their slow transit time (it takes meat about three days to be completely digested and leave the system). This slows the digestion and depletes the body of minerals. Vegetable proteins, on the other hand, fully nourish the body, being quickly and efficiently metabolized. If you have to eat meat, make sure that it is made more digestible with spices such as garlic, ginger, cumin and black pepper.

* Eat food which is high in mineral content as it keeps the body looking alive and charged with energy. Minerals greatly contribute to that intangible radiant, fresh and magnetic look of a person in good health.

* Use sattvic spices such as basil, mint, cardamom, cinnamon, coriander, cumin, fennel, fenugreek, fresh ginger and turmeric liberally in cooking and serving. Use rajasic spices such as black pepper, red pepper and garlic in small quantities.

Vihara – Lifestyle

Ayurveda lays a great deal of emphasis on routine whether it is a daily one (dinacharya) or a seasonal one (ritucharya). Routines help in harmonizing our lives with the rest of the universe. The ancient rishis considered routines to be a stronger healing force than any curative medication. Adherence to the routine prescribed by dinacharya keeps the tridoshas (vata, pitta and kapha) in a healthy state of balance. Cultivating daily rituals is an important part of living a conscious life.

* Rise early

    Arise at least 45 minutes before dawn as there is a surge of energy in the air just before dawn. The Sanskrit texts *call* this time *Brahma Muhurta* and it is believed that there is more prana and *sattva* in the air at this time. By receiving this positive influence, we can gain greater freshness, strength and inclination for work.

* Focus on your body

    Upon waking, spend a few moments focusing on your body and mind. Say a short prayer thanking the forces of nature for having given another chance to start afresh. Plan for the day ahead and avoid getting into conversations until later. Walking outside for a few minutes will help you make the most of the fresh morning air, filling the system with prana or vital energy.

* Eliminate

Establish a routine to evacuate the bowels at the same time each day and ensure that you do not consume any food or drink before emptying the bowels. Specially avoid coffee or tea first thing in the morning as they stimulate the body even before it has a chance to detoxify itself.

Also eliminate all unnecessary and negative thoughts with positive affirmations such as "Today, I will have an awesome day" or "Today, I will bring only goodness into my life."

* Cleanse

After evacuation, clean your teeth and also scrape the tongue with a silver tongue cleaner. Wash your face with cool water. You can bathe the eyes with rose water or honey. Put three to four drops of warm ghee in nostrils. This cleanses the sinuses and improves vision and mental clarity. In dry atmosphere, it will keep the nostrils lubricated, thereby keeping infections away. Gargle with herbs such as mint water or neem water or coconut oil. This strengthens gums and teeth and also prevents bad breath.

* Choose your sensory inputs

Our surroundings are constantly bombarding us with negativity. Newspapers and television channels highlight all the things that are wrong with the world and the message we send to our minds is that nothing is right, lawful or fair anymore. This is far from the truth. We are actually living in the best of times, with fewer wars and lesser number of poor people than ever before in history. Be judicious in your choice of reading, television programmes, browsing the internet and in interactions with people. Avoid news items and films with violence and seek content such as meaningful documentaries and stories that nourish the soul.

* Maintain pleasant human relationships with minimal friction

    One of the most fulfilling aspects of living is to have meaningful, loving relationships. Avoid holding grudges and words spoken in anger are best forgotten. Remember that it is OK to be angry but it is never OK to be cruel. Words spoken in anger can be very hurtful so in situations when you are anger, remain silent whatever be the provocation. Nourish the relationships with family and friends by being a good listener and having empathy. It is very easy to judge people so avoid the temptation to affix labels.

* Live in harmony with the rhythms of the day and seasons

    Regulate the daily events of waking up, eating and sleeping at similar times each day. Make sure to get enough sleep (6–8 hours) on most days. Increase interaction with nature. Go for a walk in a park or by a lake whenever possible, taking in the surroundings with keen interest and observation.

* Exercise

    Indulge in some form of exercise at least 6 days of the week. Walking for 45 minutes each day would be ideal. However, if you do not have the time, you can split it into 4 sessions of 10 minutes each. You can also practice some asanas which will lend your body strength and flexibility. Learn how to do the Surya Namaskar as it provides a whole body workout.

* Meditate

    Meditation is a wonderful way of centring the body, mind and soul and contrary to popular belief, it is very simple and easy to do. Meditation leaves you feeling more calm, balanced, creative and healthy. You can start meditating by merely focusing on your breath and noting the thoughts that flit past your mind.

    The idea behind meditation is not to have a completely blank mind but to clear the mind of thoughts for that time alone. Just watching your thoughts and not zeroing in on one thought and letting go of the thought once it has arisen in the mind is one of the ways of meditating.

You can also use a mantra or an affirmation to bring yourself into a meditative frame of mind. It is also very important to meditate on the thought of death each day. This will help you overcome your fear of death as you slowly come to the understanding that if death comes, you will merely be shedding this mortal body.

* Abhyanga

    Apply warm oil on the head and massage the body for around ten minutes at least once a week. Massage promotes healing by releasing toxins, increasing blood flow and delivering nutrients to all the parts of the body. Self-massage also helps make us more aware of our own bodies. Take a bath after the Abhyanga but avoid the use of soap as all soaps contain animal fats which only deplete the skin of necessary oils.

    Once a week, use a good exfoliant (such as besan mixed with sugar crystals) to remove all dead tissues. It leaves the skin feeling fresh and revitalized.

* Detoxify

    Take a teaspoonful of Triphala powder each day as it is a powerful detoxifier and also acts as a safe and gentle colon cleanser. Take a Panchakarma, Ayurveda's most potent detoxification programme from time to time. To enable your mind to let go of all the negative emotions, keep a diary recording all the thoughts and feelings. This will act as a catharsis and enable you to overcome hurt and disappointment. Forgive all those who you feel have hurt you. Do this to free yourself of all the negativity so that you can experience peace of mind.

* Care for the environment

    We have a deep and abiding relationship with the universe. It may not be very evident to us at all times but the environment is constantly influencing us and we are exercising our influence on all things around us. It is, therefore, imperative that we care for our environment.

    You can do your bit for the environment by sticking to a vegetarian diet and eating organic foods. Avoid using silks and leather products. Avoid wasting precious resources such as water, petrol and power. Limit the use of soaps and detergents and stop the use of plastic bags. Mother Teresa once said "If we cannot live for others, then the life is not worth living." Care for others and all that which surrounds you and you will be cared for and nurtured in return.

* Cultivate a Sattvic attitude

    The simplest way to cultivate a sattva is to develop a sense of gratitude. Gratitude allows us to celebrate the present by being thankful for all that we possess. It magnifies positive emotions and blocks toxic, negative emotions, such as envy, resentment, regret.

* Live mindfully and in the present moment

    Life unfolds only in the present moment yet so much of our time goes in thinking about the past or worrying about the future. Living mindfully is to be utterly present in the moment. When we anchor our awareness in the present moment, we are living life to the fullest by not letting our thoughts rule over us. Remember that the days may seem long but the years are short.

It is very easy for all of us to be deluded about our state of mindfulness. It needs a great deal of practice as it is something that develops when we give constant attention to our thoughts and actions. Many people whom I met in the course of my retreats claimed that they had mastered mindfulness. I observed that their mindfulness was limited only to the extent of their yoga or meditation class and once they stepped out in the real world, they reverted to habitual unmindful thoughts and actions.

There is a story of a mindfulness master and his pupil which explains this delusion beautifully.

A pupil approached his Zen master and expressed his desire to learn mindfulness. The master told him to practice and come back to him after seven years. At the end of seven years, the pupil went in search of the master to show him his proficiency and mastery over mindfulness. It was a rainy day when he reached the master's small hut deep inside the forest. He left his umbrella and wet shoes outside the door as he entered the hut to pay his respects to the master. The master received him warmly. The disciple was filled with pride as he announced his mastery over mindfulness. The master plainly asked him after listening to the description of all his exploits: "Did you leave your umbrella to the left or to the right side of your shoes?" The pupil was dumbstruck as he did not know the answer. He realized that in the moment of excitement of announcing his skill to his master, he had forgotten to be mindful. He then left for another seven years of practice.

Therefore, your efforts to be more sattvic in your living will lead to you to have a clear mind, with positive and pure thoughts most of the time. Your perceptions of the world around you become less judgemental as you accept people and situations for what they are, rather than what you think.

It is important to keep in mind that in your striving towards a sattvic life, you should not be overly goal-oriented or become too attached to the concepts of right and wrong and dos and don'ts of the process. If you become too dogmatic in your pursuit, then the outcome would be rajasic in nature, leading to tamas as you tire yourself needlessly by putting pressure to conform to a set of guidelines.

The key to evolving into a sattvic person lies in making small changes in your day-to-day lives which translates in big changes when they become habits. With time, these habits lead you to a life of greater balance, clarity and peace while allowing you to lead fuller lives with a heightened awareness of yourself, well-developed intuitive faculties and a sense of deep connection with the universe.

In this state of "Satchidananda," you will find that your spiritual destiny is fulfilled as you become capable of manifesting all that you truly desire to fully enjoy your life.

8

SIMPLE RITUAL WORSHIP OF THE SRI CHAKRA YANTRA

A 12 x 12 inch print out of an accurate Sri Chakra Yantra (as seen on the cover of this book) is sufficient for daily ritual worship.

If you intend to become a serious practitioner of the Sri Chakra, then I would recommend that you buy a copper yantra in 12 x 12 inches. Please check for accuracy by comparing the copper engravings against the ones in image () and go with your instinct to pick up the one that feels most right for you out of the group.

Once you bring the yantra home, keep it in a clean place and cover it with a red cloth until you take it out for use in the ritual. You can also buy a small japa mala (rosary made of tulsi beads or any other material, though the ideal one for the Sri Chakra Yantra is the one made of coral) to use it as a part of the ritual.

Choose a spot in your home or office where you wish to place the yantra. The best position would be in the north-eastern quadrant of your space with you facing east when doing the puja. Find a small wooden platform and cover it with a yellow cloth to place the yantra in a horizontal position for the puja. You can place the yantra in a vertical position during meditation.

The next step is to consecrate the yantra and infuse energy into it to make it fit for the ritual. This is called "prana pratistha." Some people call upon learned Brahmin scholars to do the pran pratishta puja but my belief is that it is better if it is done by the practitioner with devotion and sincerity.

Ideally, pran pratistha is to be done on a Friday. Check the internet or Hindu panchanga or a calender for an auspicious time on the day you intend to do the puja. The night before, ensure that you soak the yantra in water with a few crystals of salt to dissipate any negativity it may have gathered when stored in the shop.

On the day of the puja, shower and wear red clothes. Prepare a sweet dish which is yellow in colour. If you are not able to make a naivedyam, it is fine to offer bananas or any other fruit you have at home. Place the yantra on the wooden platform and adorn it with sandalwood paste on the four corners of the copper plate. Light two diyas (lamps with cotton wick and oil/ghee) on either side of the yantra. Place a few red flowers around the yantra. Light some incense sticks.

Chant the mantra 108 times:

"Om Sri Tripurasundhari Padhuka Pujyami Namah"

Imagine that your yantra has now started to get energized and with each ritual that you perform, this energy gets stronger and stronger and this highly energized yantra is your personal tool to connect with the universe whenever you need.

Do an arati using camphor and ring a bell. As this is the time you are energizing the yantra, it would also help if you can chant all the sounds associated with the Sri Chakra Yantra. This process would be a long one but will be well-worth the time spent as it further enhances your connection with the yantra while also energizing the environment around you.

You can start with the Panchadashi mantra (108 times), then follow it up with Khadgamala and Lalita Trishati. If you are a novice and do not know any of the above, it is also fine to play all of these mantras in the background as you prepare and proceed with the pooja.

Ideally, this ritual should be repeated on every Friday, full moon days and auspicious occasions such as Akshaya Tritiya, Diwali, Dusshera and your birthday. It is also useful to perform the ritual before you embark on a new journey and especially when you find yourself at the crossroads or wish to overcome a particularly difficult time in your life.

Meditation on the Sri Chakra

If you are new to any form of meditation practice, then begin by devoting 5-6 minutes every day to gazing at the Sri Chakra Yantra. Initially, do not think too much about the process or the outcome. Just focus on sitting as still as you can with your gaze at the Yantra.

In case you do not possess a copper Sri Chakra, I recommend that you use an accurate black and white representation printed on paper rather than a coloured one as colours tend to have inherent associations which we wish to avoid at this stage. I would suggest that you do not use an image on the laptop, computer screen, TV screen or mobile screen as the energy emitted by electronic devices may interfere with the energy fields.

The most ideal location is a small area dedicated to your practice. This will help you gain focus faster as your practice progresses. Choose a place to sit, preferably on the floor with a mat. You must be facing east, sitting in the north-east quadrant of your space. The Sri Chakra Yantra should be placed directly before you in the east direction at a distance of about one feet from you at eye level. You must be able to clearly discern the different lines and patterns without straining the eyes.

Begin by folding your hands in prayer and chanting Om three times to bring your mind into focus.

Focus on your breath and notice how it slows down when you observe it consciously. Allow your entire body to relax as you breathe normally but with awareness. Keep your face relaxed at all times by smiling very gently and effortlessly.

Slowly take your eyes to the bindu and let it rest there gently. Do not stare or fix your gaze tightly. Without moving your eyes, gradually take in the triangle that contains the bindu and take in the beauty of the symmetrical design. Allow your vision to expand to the next set of triangles and rest your focus on each set for as long as you are comfortable doing so. Then bring the first set of petals into focus and feel your gaze extending outward just as the petals are seen blossoming. Include the second set of petals in your line of vision and let your attention grasp the entire pattern for a while.

Now slowly recognize the three concentric circles and allow them to enter you line of vision. Slowly acknowledge the square with the four gateways and let your eyes gaze upon the entire pattern in unity. Keep your focus there for as long as you can while continuing to breathe slowly and calmly, feeling a deep sense of relaxation taking over your mind and body.

Now slowly bring your attention from the square to the circles as you proceed on an inward journey through the various shapes in the Sri Yantra. Arrive at the triangle that encloses the bindu and focus your attention there briefly before making the bindu your sole focus of attention. At this time, your gaze should almost be bringing your attention to the area between your eyebrows. Rest your gaze there as you have arrived at the point of cosmic dissolution from where creation begins again.

Slowly close your eyes and bring your attention from the bindu to your breath and keep your eyes closed as you try to visualize the yantra in your mind's eye. Sit in the same meditative position for a few minutes before gently getting up after folding your hands in the prayer position. Do not be tempted to judge your experience or be disappointed if you feel no different from before you took up the meditation.

Understand that the exercise you have undertaken is making changes in your brain and will continue to do so for as long as you remain steadfast in your practice. This change in brain structure is scientifically known as neuroplasticity and meditation has been one of the most well-accepted methods to change patterns in the brain.

The Sri Chakra Yantra is a magical tool that stimulates and concentrates the psychic forces that you engage in. In Tantra, creation and destruction are seen as a continuum and all manifestations – from the grossest to the subtlest - are eventually connected and are one and the same.

As you expand your vision from the bindu to the square, you are participating in a meditative method that involves evolution (extending outward from the centre to multiply into an array of creativity). Evolution symbolizes our gradual moving from the Divine to all the aspects of the outer world while understanding that the subtle worlds give rise to the mundane and the gross.

As you bring your attention back from the square to the bindu, you are involved in a method that is known as involution (collapsing inward from the perimetre to the centre). Involution is the moving away from the gross and dualities towards the subtle and non-dualistic reality. You dissolve all misconceptions to become one with the Divine.

The whole universe contains signs of our unity with the Divine but we miss out on these signs because of our utter ignorance. This is beautifully explained in a story from the Puranas.

There is an elderly couple living in the forest. Their life is filled with difficulty and every day is a challenge as they have to seek food and water and are at the mercy of nature. Parvathi, who is watching over the earth, notices the couple's despair and asks Shiva to do something to help them. Shiva says I have tried many times in the past but they are so caught up in their difficulties that they fail to see the signs. Parvathi insists that Shiva does something for them at that instant. Shiva manifests a large bag of coins which lands on the floor of the forest, not far from where the elderly couple are walking.

At the same time, the lady says to her husband that soon they may be blind so they should start practicing living in the forest without being able to see. They tie blindfolds on each other and walk on. The bag of gold is lying in their path but they kick it thinking it is a stone and curse it saying that the forest is not at all safe for blind people. Shiva, then, looks at Parvathi and says that humans are blinded by maya to an extent that they ignore all the signs of reality which are merely manifestations of the Divine.

How to use the Sri Chakra Yantra as a tool for Conscious Manifestation

		9th Avarana: Make a connection with the universe
		8th Avarana: Make your request with vision and clarity
		7th Avarana: Confirm your desire
		6th Avarana: Visualise the outcome in great detail
		5th Avarana: Imagine how you will feel when the desire is fulfilled
		4th Avarana: Let go of all doubts and negative thoughts
		3rd Avarana: Detach from the desire
		2nd Avarana: Be grateful and give thanks in advance
		1st Avarana: Do a quick recap of all steps

We are continuously creating our own reality – consciously or unconsciously. The reality that we unconsciously create can be unreliable as we cannot be sure that the outcome will be exactly as we desire.

Let us go back to the example at the beginning of the book about unconsciously manifesting a career out of a childhood desire. It may or may not have turned out as you desired because when you manifest unconsciously, you are governed by your beliefs, prejudices and conditioned thought patterns. As a child, if you were told by a teacher that you are no good at maths, it might turn you in the direction of commerce or humanities, simply because you believe what has been told to you. But commerce or humanities may not be what you really wanted to pursue.

Another example of unconscious manifesting can be your choice of a life partner. We all tend to go by what is expected of us by our parents or peers or society in general which may necessarily not be the qualities that we desire in our partner. We then end up making the wrong choices and unhappiness and frustration follows. Unconscious manifestation can lead to disappointment and sadness because we create our realities without being completely aware of what we seek.

Conscious manifestation, on the other hand, is all about clarity and involves explicitly expressing to the universal energy what it is that you truly, strongly and deeply desire. It is not enough to merely desire something. You must invest in it your emotions and feelings to make it a reality. There has to be a passion in your desire, not just an apathetic wanting. Once you are clear about what you desire and state it, it is time to sit back and trust the universe to deliver. It is very important that you trust the process and not harbour doubts about "how" it will happen.

For example, you desire a four-bedroom house with a small garden in a specific area in your city. Do not think for a moment – "where will I get the money to buy it?" or "will I be able to maintain such a big house?" These doubts will only negate the entire process of conscious manifestation as they create confusion about whether you are worthy of it or really desire it in the first place. Keep the eyes and ears open to any opportunities but never doubt that the house of your dreams will be yours soon.

Here are a few guidelines to help manifest consciously:

1. Have a clear vision of what you desire. You must know with clarity exactly what it is that you are seeking. If it is a material object, then be as specific as you can about size, shape, colour and features. If you wish to see yourself as a published author, then have a vision of how the book will look. If you are seeking enhancement of a skill, then outline in what area you wish to see growth.

2. Energize your vision by stating it to yourself and by focussing on it several times a day for just a few seconds. This way you are strengthening your desire by focusing your attention on it again and again. Where attention goes, energy flows in that direction.

3. Make your intention clear to the universe and to yourself. You can do this in any number of creative ways. In ancient pagan rituals, the desires were written out on bay leaves or rocks and caves. You can write your desires down carefully and consciously and store it in a safe place.

4. Take the necessary actions required to create your vision. Obviously some action is needed from your end to acquire what you desire. You will need to be on the lookout for that four-bedroom house or complete the manuscript of the book. You will need to be fully aware and awake to the possibilities of coincidences and serendipity bringing you in touch with people and situations that can make your dream a reality.

5. Visualize deeply and imagine that what you seek is already yours. If you are seeking a promotion then imagine what it would be like to be seated in your new office, with all the added perks that come with the position. Visualize yourself as dressed in better clothes, carrying yourself with greater confidence and leading people in your company. The greater your sense of visualization, the better will be your ability to manifest.

6. Clear all negative thoughts. Believe and trust the universe. You will have several moments when you will think "Ah, this is not going to work" or "I don't deserve this." Keep such thoughts out while focussing on thinking that miracles do happen and that

you could be at the receiving end. You have nothing to lose and everything to gain with this positive mindset.

7. Surrender to the process. Once you have decided to trust the universe, develop a sense of detachment from the desire and allow your mind to be free of thoughts which will keep arising about the how and the when. Just know and be secure in your ability to manifest and bide your time. There is no time frame in which the manifestation will occur so be patient.

8. Give thanks. Even before you see the results of your created reality, get into a grateful state of mind and remember to thank the universe for offering you the opportunity to collaborate in the creative process.

While meditating on the Sri Chakra Yantra, focus on the various avaranas at different stages of your manifestation process.

As you begin the process, meditate on the 1st avarana to help make the connection with the universe. Meditation at this level also helps you to be more grounded in your own self and will guide you intuitively to make the right decisions.

You now have a vision and clarity about what you seek. It is time to make the request to the universe. Take your attention to the 2nd avarana and state clearly what you desire with specific outcomes that you have in mind.

Allow a day or two before moving on to strengthening and further clarifying your desire as you meditate upon the 3rd avarana. Reiterate your idea and confirm it in your mind as you keep your eyes focussed on the 8 petals pattern.

By now, you should be visualizing the outcome in detail. If your desire is a material one, then imagine it with all its qualities including colour, shape and size. If your desire is an intangible one such as an entrepreneurial endeavour, then visualize your business plan with as much detail as possible. Imagine a buzzing office with staff, see your website being created and visualize yourself signing business deals. Focus on the 4th avarana with your eyes moving along the triangles starting from the left in the clockwise direction.

Spend some time each day meditating on the outcome. Imagine how you will feel when your desire is fulfilled. Visualize your reaction and notice how you will feel in mind, body and spirit. Feel the excitement and the joy of the moment and allow yourself to enjoy this sensation. The brain does not know the real from the imaginary so just soak in the feeling as your eyes wander over the triangles of the 5th avarana.

While meditating on the 6th avarana, let go of all the doubts and negative thoughts that might slip into your mind and distance you from your dream. As the triangles get smaller, allow your focus to get more intense and continue to visualize an outcome that exactly matches with your desire.

As you approach the bindu, the point of universal creativity, begin to detach yourself from your desire. This does not mean letting go of your vision but implies instead that you now have implicit faith in the universe and you surrender with trust. Focus your eyes on the small triangles of the 7th avarana and express your sense of wonder and excitement at what is to come.

Approach the 8th avarana with a sense of immense gratitude and give thanks in advance to the process of creation. Gratitude generates positive emotions and helps improve all aspects of our life – health, abundance and relationships. It also helps you appreciate what you already have and prepares you to receive more into your life.

You are now finally at the bindu, the vortex of creation itself, and now as you meditate upon the dot at the centre of the triangle, do a quick recap of all the steps from making the connection to visualizing to strengthening and finally letting go and giving thanks. At this point, intensify your meditation yet again and ask that your actions be fuelled by the Universal energy and spend a few minutes with your eyes closed appreciating the calmness of the moment.

Mircea Eliade wrote that there are two distinct ways of being – the sacred and the profane. The sacred way of being involves our looking at the world with awe and fascination, marvelling at the mysteries that remain locked in the universe. The profane way of being is living our lives without ever wondering about the magic or the mystery of the universe.

Let us use the Sri Chakra Yantra as a tool to connect us to the sacred for it temporarily disengages us from our role in the profane world of humdrum existence and helps us enter into a zone to connect more closely with the sacred. Let us allow the Sri Chakra Yantra to motivate us, help us fulfil our deepest desires and create as well as sustain our unique identity in this crowded planet.

Meditation for good health and curing specific ailments

As seen in the chapter, Sri Chakra and the human body, both are merely representations of each other – one depicting the macrocosm and the other the microcosm of the Universal energy.

Our body is an embodiment of the energy that resides in the Sri Chakra and as such, we can all be seen as having our own individual Sri Chakra that is represented by our bodies. As a result of our karma in past life and actions in present life, our Sri Chakra undergoes distortion and damage and moves away from the perfection of the universal Sri Chakra. This imperfection gives rise to ill health and disease(s). By taking steps to purify our Sri Chakra by way of adopting sattvic practices, including rituals in our everyday life and connecting with the universal energy, we can correct these distortions and imperfections and move towards better health and wellbeing.

The Sri Chakra Yantra also has the unique ability to allow us to raise our vibratory level. It is said that lower vibratory levels (a result of anger, hate, greed, jealousy, etc.,) lead to disease, pain and depression, and higher vibratory levels (a result of gratitude, love, compassion, etc.,) promote a pain-free life filled with positivity and joy.

The chart below depicts various avaranas upon which meditation can be undertaken to help treat specific ailments. The seventh enclosure, consisting of eight triangles, is the Sarva Rogahara Chakra or one that is the Remover of all Diseases. Focussing your attention on this avarana will endow you with a healing energy to overcome chronic diseases and painful afflictions besides building immunity and keeping the body youthful and full of energy.

Sri Chakra Yantra

	**9th Avarana:**	Knee pain, Any joint pain, Alzheimer, Parkinson's
	8th Avarana:	Infertility, Sexual disorders
	7th Avarana:	Ulcers, Digestive issues, Irritable bowel syndrome, Gall bladder stone
▲	**6th Avarana:**	Heart disease, Low and high blood pressure
▲	**5th Avarana:**	Skin, Sinus, Lungs, Shoulder pain, Spondylitis
▲	**4th Avarana:**	Psychological disorders, Schizophrenia, Suicidal thoughts
▲	**3rd Avarana:**	To rid oneself of all ailments
▼	**2nd Avarana:**	To cleanse and purify all
○	**1st Avarana:**	Overcome sense of self, addictions, greed and find connection with Universal healing power

REFERENCES

1. The Sri Chakra as a symbol of the human body – P.R. Krishna Kumar
2. Sri Vidya and Sri Chakra – Lalithananda Lalita Prasad Jammulamadaka
3. Sri Yantra – Bernhard Wimmer
4. Devi's names and locations in Sri Chakra Navavarana puja – Ramani's Blog
5. Sri Yantra Research Centre
6. Sri Yantra – Gerard Huet
7. How to harness the power of Sri Yantra – Gaia
8. How to meditate with Sri Yantra – Davidji
9. Yantra, the tantric symbol of cosmic unity – Madhu Khanna
10. Symbolism of the Sri Yantra – Rohit Arya
11. Sri Yantra – Dhyana Foundation
12. Sri Chakra – Sreenivasa Rao's blogs
13. Sri Yantra and Sri Vidya healing – Dr. B. Sreejahanathan
14. The Tantra of Sri Chakra Bhavanopanishad – Prof. S.K. Ramachandra Rao
15. The great goddess Lalitha and the Sri Chakra – Subhash Kak
16. Sri Vidya Sadhana – Sri Sivapremanandaji

17. International Journal of Geology, Agriculture and Environmental Sciences, Vol 5 Issue 2
18. The Fantastic Science of Yantra – Swami Satyanand Saraswati
19. The Mahavidyas – Devadatta Kali (Vedanta Society of California)
20. Shakti and Shakta – Avalon Arthur
21. Ten Great Cosmic Powers – S. Sankarnarayanan
22. Sri Devi Khadgamala – Sri Amrita Ananda
23. Mantra Yoga and Primal Sound – Dr. David Frawley
24. Understanding and Worshipping Sri Chakra – V Ravi
25. Hindupedia
26. The Sacred and the Profane: The Nature of Religion: The Significance of Religious Myth, Symbolism, and Ritual within Life and Culture – Mircea Eliade
27. Hridaya Yoga – Antonotea Gotea

ACKNOWLEDGEMENTS

I want to say thank you to the people in my life who listened to me without judgement, spoke without prejudice, supported without entitlement, understood without pretence and loved without conditions.

I owe everything to them.

My gurus – Dr. Talavane Krishna and Sri David Aitken

My mentors – Sri P.V. Giri, Smt. Chaya Venkatesh and Dr. C.S. Venkatesh

My parents - Sri S.P. Narayana Rao and Smt Devi and my brother Nandu Siddoji Rao

My late parents-in-law - Sri R.S. Krishnaji Rao and Smt Vanamala

My husband Raj for his unflinching support in all my endeavours

My daughter Puja and son-in-law Amit who are the fulcrum of my existence

My soul-sisters Swaroopa, Kiran, Rakhee, Ameeta, Sona and Upasna

My dear friend, business partner and the catalyst behind this book, Sri Sanjay Soni

Printed in Great Britain
by Amazon